# WITCHCRAFT

## • A MODERN GUIDE •

# WITCHCRAFT

## • A MODERN GUIDE •

A PRACTICAL HANDBOOK FOR BEGINNERS AND BEYOND

ALESTREL EVERGREEN

For our Great Mother.
May she always protect us;
may we always honor her.

First published 2021

Exisle Publishing Pty Ltd
PO Box 864, Chatswood, NSW 2057, Australia
226 High Street, Dunedin, 9016, New Zealand
www.exislepublishing.com



Conceived, designed, and produced by
The Bright Press,
an imprint of The Quarto Group
The Old Brewery, 6 Blundell Street,
London N7 9BH, United Kingdom.
(0)20 7700 6700
www.QuartoKnows.com



A CiP catalogue record for this book is available from the National Library of Australia.

ISBN 978-1-922539-22-9

Publisher: James Evans
Editorial Director: Isheeta Mustafi
Art Director: James Lawrence
Managing Editor: Jacqui Sayers
Editor: Emily Angus
Project Editor: Anna Southgate
Design: Matt Windsor
Layout: Paul Sloman

2 4 6 8 10 9 7 5 3 1

While every care has been taken in presenting this material, the information should be taken at the reader's own risk. Neither the author nor the publisher may be held responsible for any type of damage or harm resulting from the content of this book or that caused by the use or misuse of information from any activities in this book.

If you need medical, physical, or mental help please consult a doctor. Readings do not substitute for medical advice or treatment.

# CONTENTS

# AN INTRODUCTION TO WITCHCRAFT

*Two women consult with a witch in this Roman mosaic from the Villa of Cicero, Pompeii, currently at the National Archaeological Museum in Naples, Italy.*

The term "witchcraft" is well over a thousand years old, and the concept of a person—generally a woman—who was wise in the ways of herbs and healing is much older still. The origin of the word "witch" is uncertain: most Anglo-Saxon dictionaries note an Old English form, *wicce*, meaning "witch" or "sorceress." Another, similar, Anglo-Saxon word, *wice*, which means "to bend or shape" (as in wickerwork, the bending and shaping of hazel or willow twigs to make useful items such as baskets), may be a more accurate etymology, given that one aim of witchcraft is to shape the forces of the natural world by will.

## WITCHCRAFT TRADITIONS

Essentially, witchcraft is the practice of using the natural forces of the world to accomplish specific aims. There are many different ways to do this, and we will be exploring some of them in this book.

Witchcraft has been viewed both positively and negatively over the ages. At the beginning of the last millennium, it was used of the wise woman of the village, the one who had studied herbs and herbal remedies and was able to advise her neighbors of ways to improve their health. In later times, it was associated with black magic and denigrated as evil; practitioners were often imprisoned, tortured, and hanged or burned to death. The dark, malevolent image of the witch remains popular right up to the present day, although there has been a more positive shift since the turn of the 21st century. Fortunately, these days, we are somewhat more enlightened, and although the term "witch" can still raise a shudder in some places, the practice is now generally accepted as a lifestyle or religion choice in the form of Wicca.

This book offers an introduction to traditional witchcraft. For the purposes of this book, those who practice are referred to as the Wise, their practice is known as the Craft, and our personal journey to learn and use the Craft is called the Path.

Welcome to a bright new path, and may your journey be blessed with tremendous joy and success!

# A BRIEF HISTORY OF WITCHCRAFT

*The archetypal witch is the Halloween kind, who flies on a broomstick in the dead of night, dressed in a pointed hat and with a black cat by her side.*

## WITCHES' COVENS

From its earliest beginnings as a form of herbalism and primitive medicine, the Craft of the Wise—the Old Ways, as it was called back then—grew and developed into a rather more complicated entity. Having originally been a solitary practice, over time the Craft became more organized. Like-minded individuals found each other, and met and traded secrets and information in groups that became known, eventually, as covens.

*A depiction of witches being burned at the stake in Derenburg, Germany, from the* Derenburg Zeitung, *1555.*

A coven is anything from a minimum of three people upward. The much-maligned coven of thirteen—twelve witches and their leader, the devil, as a mockery of the Christian twelve disciples and Jesus—is a 20th-century invention. There is no devil in witchcraft traditions. Instead he is a concept of the Abrahamic religions (Judaism, Christianity, Islam) and has no place in the Craft of the Wise, although there are those who consider Lucifer the Morning Star to be the bringer of knowledge and understanding to humankind, and honor him as such. The modern image of the Christian devil, horned, goat-legged, and cloven-hoofed, is taken from the far more ancient image of Pan, Cernunnos, and the Horned God.

Sometimes the traditions of the Wise were passed down through generations of the same family. Such "hereditary witches" may have been born into the family, but membership isn't automatic; each family member must learn the Craft and make a conscious decision to be accepted.

Following brutal purges, lasting from the 15th to the 18th centuries, witchcraft became more secretive. In the United Kingdom, the Witchcraft Law, passed in 1735, abolished the hunting and execution of supposed witches, but made the practice of witchcraft illegal and punishable by a year's imprisonment. The law wasn't repealed until more than 200 years later, in 1951.

## TOWARD WICCA

What is now known as Wicca started in England and dates back to 1954 when its founder, Gerald Gardner, pioneered a return to respecting and honoring the natural world, the Threefold Goddess and the Horned God, and spiritual enlightenment through means other than those of the Abrahamic religions.

It was at this point that the Craft of the Wise finally assumed its long-awaited legitimacy in the eyes of the world as a whole, and it was, to some extent, safe to call oneself a witch again, although there will always be some prejudice against the Wise from those who are afraid, intolerant, or jealous. It's often prudent to keep your beliefs to yourself until you know who you're speaking to. Similar groups to the Wiccans began to arise, including the Neo-Pagans, who followed the Craft of the Wise, but refused to use the term witch.

Gardnerian Wicca is highly formalized and hierarchical, and requires its practitioners to be initiated by someone qualified and already in the movement. Alexandrian Wicca, a sister religion to Gardnerian and founded in the 1960s, also requires initiation, but is generally less formal and structured. Both require their members to keep the belief systems, knowledge, and traditions of their Craft secret from outsiders.

*A green ceramic Mother Earth figure sits at the center of this pagan altar.*

What is now known as Correllian Wicca in the United States started as a nativist system, incorporating the traditions of indigenous Americans into European witchcraft and spiritualism, and promoting the rights of the natives over those of immigrants. Its founder was Orpheis Caroline High Correll, who claimed she was a descendant of the Cherokee Didanvwisgi (traditional healers and spiritual leaders) who had intermarried with Scottish witches. The system became known as Correllian Wicca in the 1990s. Its emphasis on native traditions and the rights of indigenous peoples was in line with the overall beliefs of Wiccans in respecting the planet and all her people.

## THE CHURCH OF THELEMA

*The unicursal hexagram is an important symbol in occult traditions, and represents macrocosmic forces. Aleister Crowley modified the symbol for his religion of Thelema, placing a five-petaled flower at the center.*

Aleister Crowley, born in 1875, was a man of many talents—poet, artist, ceremonial magician, novelist, and occultist. Something of an infamous figure, he was an outspoken social critic. He was the founder and creator of the church and religion of Thelema (Greek "will," "want," "purpose"). The basic tenets of Thelema are "Do what thou wilt shall be the whole of the Law," followed by "Love is the Law, Love under Will." Since this can be read as a selfish version of the Wiccan rede (see p. 20; it omits the "an' it harm none" and does not specify what sort of love is meant), it has caused a lot of argument and opposition in the past. The Church of Thelema is highly structured and initiatory, with a wide variety of different rules for different levels of the hierarchy within it. Thelemites worship a number of different deities, many of them from Egyptian mythology, takes elements from the Qabalah (a school of thought and discipline in Jewish mysticism), and considers everyone to have a guardian angel.

The Craft of the Wise is thus an ancient craft with a turbulent history. Currently practicing the Craft is very much easier and safer than it has been in the past. Of course, that may change. Life, after all, is change, growth, and learning if we are not to stagnate.

# WITCHCRAFT TODAY

## WITCHCRAFT TODAY

Unless you were born into a family of hereditary witches (and even then there's no hard-and-fast rule to say you can't explore and expand the Craft), today, pretty much anything is acceptable in the Craft of the Wise, as long as it causes no harm to anyone or anything else. It is important to have some knowledge of the history and traditions of the basics of the Craft, but after that, it is up to each individual to decide how to practice. The Path can be an instinctive, compulsive calling, or a conscious decision to explore and experiment with the forces around and within you.

## CONSIDER YOUR OPTIONS

You may perceive the Craft as a way to rebalance, or fight against, the overly mechanical, technological state of "civilized" society, seeking out a quieter, less damaging way of life, one that may actually improve matters.

Perhaps you wish to use the Craft as a way to increase your self-confidence and self-worth, to overcome the constraints a predominantly male-dominated society has placed on you—and this can apply wherever you are on the gender spectrum. The Craft is open and welcomes anyone, regardless of gender, color, creed, or inclination (as long as it causes no harm to anyone.)

Above and opposite: Rituals and spellwork continue to play a role in the Craft.

You may find it the best way to find yourself, to learn who you are and what you want out of life, and how to achieve it without damaging anyone or anything in the process. Maybe you would like to be a solitary witch practicing alone, often not following any particular form of the Craft but creating your own rituals and traditions based on what you are most in tune with at any given time.

Perhaps you are one of those who has a natural, instinctive understanding of the natural forces that are so much a part of the Craft—maybe even skills acquired in previous lives, if you are a believer in reincarnation. While the idea of reincarnation isn't explicit in the Craft of the Wise, belief in, and focus on, the natural cycle of birth-life-death-rebirth certainly implies it.

You may feel an attraction to a particular aspect of the traditional deities, or you may decide the Path of secular magic is better for you, honoring and respecting the forces of the world as simply that: natural forces that can be employed to work natural magic without any reference to a deity.

*Practicing witchcraft encourages a greater awareness of Nature's cycles.*

## JOINING A RELIGIOUS GROUP

Should you decide, once you have learned what is involved in the Craft, that a more structured, hierarchical form is right for you, investigate the recognized Wiccan religions—Thelema, Gardnerian, Alexandrian, and Corellian are currently the best known. The first three require initiation and hence a firm commitment to their Path. Contact details and books are available online.

## A MORE RELAXED APPROACH

You may decide to be open about your Path, happy to discuss the Craft with anyone you meet, and pleased to wear clothing, makeup, and jewelry that show your affiliations in the way that is currently believed by your society. In the West, the "Goth" look—black clothing, makeup, and a generally dark, brooding attitude—has often been assumed to reveal a connection with witchcraft, whether intended by the wearer or not. Alternatively, you may prefer to keep your association with the Craft downplayed or even secret. It's a matter of personal choice, but you are learning the Craft of the Wise, and it's only sensible not to take too many risks. The middle way is to wear a piece of jewelry that most people won't notice or understand unless they are familiar with the Craft, and that incorporates a simple Goddess or God symbol.

*Wiccan religions rely on a range of different tools and rituals to work magic.*

It is always helpful to learn a little about other forms of magic around the world. It gives a broader perspective, and you may find elements that instinctively appeal to you and can be incorporated into your own Path. Take advantage of all the resources available—books, TV programs about other versions of the Craft and about the state of the planet. Make use of the Internet, too. Use it for what it was originally intended: communication, connection, and the sharing of information.

*Consider choosing your own tools and talismans. The more personal they are, the more effective they are likely to be.*

Whichever Path appeals to you, read this book, learn what is possible, gather the few tools that are absolutely necessary, and start your journey. You'll learn a little about witchcraft and a lot about yourself along the way.

# HOW TO USE THIS BOOK

**Welcome to the start of your exploration into the ancient and venerable Craft of the Wise! It's an exciting journey, filled with insights into the Old Ways of traditional wise women (and people of any gender), ways to live life in tune with the natural ways of Mother Earth, and even suggestions for incantations to inspire you to work your own magic.**

The Craft of the Wise uses the Wheel of the Year—from the Imbolc sabbat at the start of spring, through the midwinter solstice to the Yule sabbat and back to Imbolc—and the different parts of this book follow much the same pattern, including the basics of witchcraft, both modern and traditional. Read the book through to start with, to give you a basic knowledge of the Craft. You may find it helpful to read the individual parts in Part 1 and the companion pages in Part 2 together.

Please take the information offered here and make it your own. Expand, explore, and experiment, and enjoy crafting your own Path.

## PART I: WHAT IS WITCHCRAFT?

An introduction to the Craft, covering all the basics: common deities, sacred spaces, the traditional tools, the festivals, and rules that should be followed to keep all safe.

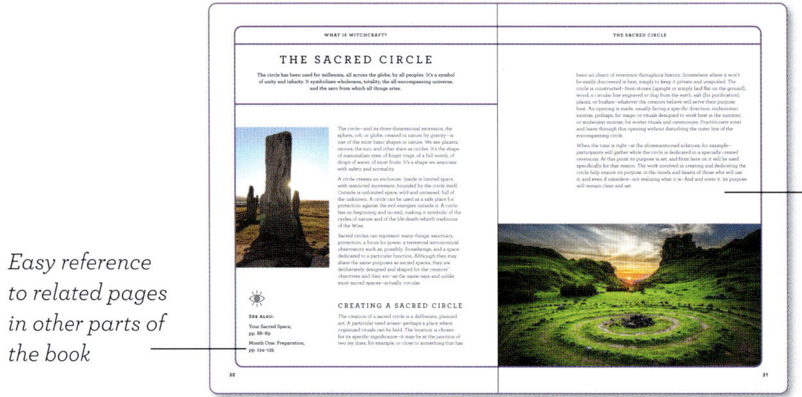
WHAT IS WITCHCRAFT?

THE SACRED CIRCLE

**The circle has been used for millennia, all across the globe, by all peoples. It's a symbol of unity and infinity. It symbolizes wholeness, totality, the all-encompassing universe, and the zero from which all things arise.**

The circle—and its three-dimensional extension, the sphere, orb, or globe, created in nature by gravity—is one of the most basic shapes in nature. We see planets, moons, the sun, and other stars as circles. It's the shape of mammalian eyes, of finger rings, of a full womb, of drops of water, of most fruits. It's a shape we associate with safety and normality.

A circle creates an enclosure. Inside is limited space, with restricted movement, bounded by the circle itself. Outside is unlimited space, wild and untamed, full of the unknown. A circle can be used as a safe place for protection against the evil energies outside it. A circle has no beginning and no end, making it symbolic of the cycles of nature and of the life-death-rebirth traditions of the Wise.

Sacred circles can represent many things: sanctuary, protection, a focus for power, a terrestrial astronomical observatory such as, possibly, Stonehenge, and a space dedicated to a particular function. Although they may share the same purposes as sacred spaces, they are deliberately designed and shaped for the creators' objectives and they are—as the name says and unlike most sacred spaces—actually circular.

SEE ALSO:

Your Sacred Space, pp. 88–89

Month One: Preparation, pp. 134–135

CREATING A SACRED CIRCLE

The creation of a sacred circle is a deliberate, planned act. A particular need arises—perhaps a place where organized rituals can be held. The location is chosen for its specific significance—it may be at the junction of two ley lines, for example, or close to something that has

30

THE SACRED CIRCLE

been an object of reverence throughout history. Somewhere where it won't be easily discovered is best, simply to keep it private and unspoiled. The circle is constructed—from stones (upright or simply laid flat on the ground), wood, a circular line engraved or dug from the earth, salt (for purification), plants, or bushes—whatever the creators believe will serve their purpose best. An opening is made, usually facing a specific direction: midsummer sunrise, perhaps, for magic or rituals designed to work best in the summer, or midwinter sunrise, for winter rituals and ceremonies. Practitioners enter and leave through this opening without disturbing the outer line of the encompassing circle.

When the time is right—at the aforementioned solstices, for example—participants will gather while the circle is dedicated in a specially created ceremony. At this point its purpose is set, and from here on it will be used specifically for that reason. The work involved in creating and dedicating the circle help ensure its purpose in the minds and hearts of those who will use it, and even if outsiders—not realizing what it is—find and enter it, its purpose will remain clear and set.

31

*Easy reference to related pages in other parts of the book*

*Text offers and overview of each subject covered and discusses the role it plays in the Craft*

## PART 2: PRACTICING WITCHCRAFT

This section provides guidance and suggestions on how to bring the Craft into your own life, how to live without harming others or our Mother Earth, and how to use the Craft to empower and energize yourself.

*Instruction and exercises based on the subjects covered in Part 1*

*Tasks for incorporating the Craft into your daily life*

## PART 3: YOUR WITCHCRAFT YEAR

This section contains ways of weaving the celebrations into your life, and using them to enliven and inspire you.

*A month-by-month program for working with the Craft*

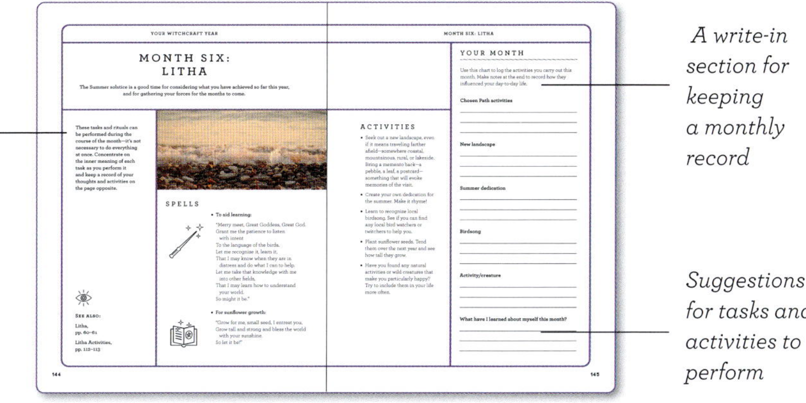


*A write-in section for keeping a monthly record*

*Suggestions for tasks and activities to perform*

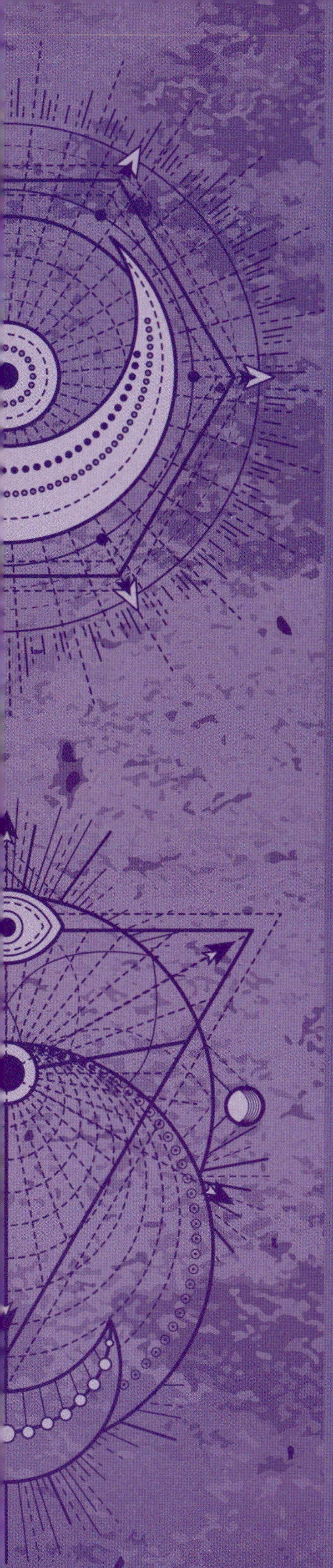

PART 1

# WHAT IS WITCHCRAFT?

# WITCHCRAFT BASICS

Introducing three key elements of witchcraft: the Wiccan rede, the threefold law, and spellwork.

## THE WICCAN REDE

"An' it harm none, do what thou will." This sentence expresses the moral precept by which all practitioners of the Craft should live. Essentially, it means that you can do what you will—"will" here meaning both "want" and "within your willpower"—as long as it causes no conscious harm, of any kind, to any other person, animal, or natural thing, including the planet. The first half of this sentence tends to be downplayed in modern times, but it's the most important precept of the Craft.

A slightly different version of the Wiccan rede was used by Aleister Crowley, English occultist and founder of the religion of Thelema: "Do what thou will shall be the whole of the law." It was followed by two other statements: "Love is the law, love under will" and "Every man and woman is a star." While this is said to mean the same as the rede, it has been used as an excuse for selfish behavior by those not familiar with Crowley's Thelemic traditions.

"Rede" means "counsel," rather than "rule." First appearing in published form in 1964, this is a Wiccan version of the golden rule: "Do as you would be done by," a version of which appears in most religions the world over. Doctors have something similar in their Hippocratic Oath: "First, do no harm."

**SEE ALSO:**

Getting Started, pp. 80–81

Your Witchcraft Year, pp. 132–133

It's relatively easy not to cause harm to yourself, but what if what you want to do harms someone else? Take the example of helping yourself to something from a large store—that is, shoplifting or stealing. It won't hurt the store, but there are always consequences. If enough people do it, the store will put its prices up to make up the shortfall, and every shopper suffers as a result. Letting off fireworks is a fun thing to do, and on special days when it's an accepted practice, no harm is done. But letting them off on other days, when they aren't expected and no one is prepared for the noise, can terrify the local pets and anyone of a nervous disposition.

And does doing what you want to do harm the planet? Best to rethink what you want and plan to make it beneficial rather than detrimental! We are all responsible for the consequences of our actions. Let's make them positive rather than negative.

## THE THREEFOLD LAW

The Craft version of karma, the threefold law states that whatever energy we put into our actions, activities, or speech—positive or negative—will be returned to us threefold (hence why keeping to the Wiccan rede is, even selfishly speaking, a good idea).

This may not work in an obvious way. Giving to charity with the expectation of receiving some sort of reward from the world at large is likely to result in disappointment. Doing so with no expectation may, and surprisingly often does, however, result in us receiving some unexpected benefit. For example, you might find extra cash in your account, gifted to you by someone quite out of the blue. Or perhaps a friend or neighbor offers, without being asked, to help you with a major task you can't accomplish by yourself. Sometimes it can be something as simple as giving a smile to someone who looks sad as you pass in the street, and being greeted with a surprised smile in return, that leaves you—and them—feeling happier knowing that someone cares. Even the smallest of helpful acts can have interesting and positive results if you are tuned in to recognize them.

On the other hand, doing harm will also have a threefold return. Spread nasty rumors about someone, or troll them online? Expect to lose friends, benefits, and maybe even your job—especially these days when so much information is public and there are so many different ways to uncover identities. Continually abuse, threaten, or belittle your child? Don't be surprised when they disown you. Deliberately steal or damage someone's property? No one is above the law—man-made or natural. There is always retribution, even if it may take a while to happen! Best to hold fast to the rede and be the best person you can be. It's a safer, happier option.

**SEE ALSO:**

Getting Started, pp. 82–83

Your Witchcraft Year, pp. 132–133

## SPELLWORK

A spell—incantation, enchantment, charm, or bewitchment—is a magical, ritual formula or action designed to produce a tangible result. It can take many forms: a spoken thought; a chanted word, sentence, or verse; an inscription; runes (pictured above) or sigils on paper, wax, sand, or stone; the creation, in wax or on paper, of the image of what is desired; or by physical action (such as lighting a candle for a person to ease their sorrows.

Much like the prayers of the religiously minded, the effectiveness of spells is debateable. A spell or prayer for rain may or may not work, depending on the weather forecast. A spell or prayer for money may or may not work, but doesn't hurt (unless we then expect it to happen and overspend what we actually have). Strictly speaking, while an incantation, prayer, or plea to the universe for something good to happen doesn't harm anyone, it's best not to expect it to come true. If it then does, even better!

That said, ending a ritual with a blessing or a little spell for success is a pleasant, traditional, ceremonial way of bringing the rite to a close. Our own spells can take any form we like, but it is an old custom to end a spoken spell with the words, "So might it be"—an appeal to any powers that may be listening, or to our own determination, to make the spell successful. There will be examples of spells for you to try in Parts Two and Three of this book.

# THE ROLE OF NATURE

**Much witchcraft relies on the natural world and the harmonious balance of its cycles.**

We have just one planet, a beautiful, vital, little green, blue, gold, and white orb spinning around a very ordinary star in a vast, vast universe. It gave us birth over eons, and has nurtured us throughout its long, long history. Without it we would not exist. There are, no doubt, many other planets in the universe, and it's more than likely that many, if not all of them contain life of some kind—we know life exists in the most unlikely of environments even on Earth—but the distances and technology involved in simply seeing them make it unlikely that we'll ever contact them, let alone be able to visit or colonize them (unless some way to exceed the speed of light can be found or invented). Even our closest neighbors—the moon and Mars—are uninhabitable by humans without major technological interventions, and while we may dream of traveling to Mars and living there, at present the difficulties look pretty insurmountable, certainly for the bulk of humanity. It makes perfect sense, then, to look after this world. It's the only one most of us will ever have.

## THE NATURAL WORLD

It's obvious to anyone that humans have not treated their home world very well. We've managed to pollute just about everything there is to pollute, and the inequalities that cause so many of our problems show no signs of being corrected any time soon. However, there is always hope, and we can improve life on our planet if we have the will to do so.

Our natural world is beautiful, invigorating, intriguing, and a great healer—of herself and the creatures living on her—but all things need to be in balance. Natural cycles

**SEE ALSO:**

Embracing Nature, pp. 84–87

Month Four: Time for Action, pp. 140–141

are created and kept in rhythm by the forces that surround us: the seasons, the weather, day into night back into day, birth, growth, decay and death, to be reborn into a new day. We are at our best when we follow these rhythms, dancing and rejoicing in them, and when we keep ourselves, as well as everything around us, in balance.

From the tallest, most majestic trees to the humblest of living flora, green algae, we know that all plants take in carbon dioxide and release it as the oxygen we need to breathe. Cutting down large swathes of forest or destroying beneficial species of algae reduces the amount of oxygen produced as well as leading to problems such as soil erosion and local changes in the weather. The recent drive to replant forests is a great way to reverse the damage, although it needs to be taken up globally to truly work. We are all connected to—and by—the natural world, and must all take responsibility for her health and well-being.

## THE NATURE OF THE WISE

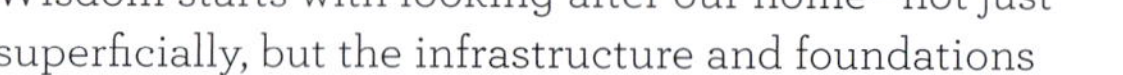

Wisdom starts with looking after our home—not just superficially, but the infrastructure and foundations too; indeed, these aspects should come first. The same is true of us as individuals. A healthy body, a curious, appreciative, tolerant mind, and a compassionate, empathic spirit are the right of every human, but unfortunately these qualities are rather difficult to find in a world that is often intolerant and selfish. We can achieve such goals—it's just going to take a bit of work.

### GREEN LIVING

When it comes to our bodies, something that helps both us and our planet is to eat only organically grown and eco-friendly fruits, vegetables, and carbohydrates (bread, lentils, beans), and organically bred, kindly treated, and humanely slaughtered animals. We should also use only recycled and reusable commodities. But since, at present, such a lifestyle is prohibitively expensive, we should do the best we can. Switching one or two items to recycled, edibles to organic and/or locally grown, and buying less plastic every month is achievable and helps our overall health. Not only that, but the cash goes to help ethically run businesses as they work hard to improve our way of life and the planet.

It can be difficult to change and improve ingrained habits, opinions, and attitudes, especially if they have been with us since childhood. It takes time, and a lot of introspective self-examination, but if we are sincere in our wish to become one of the Wise, and travel our own Path, it is important. Starting out with a vengeful spirit is anything but wise. Always remember, though, that none of us is perfect. We will sometimes fail, or backtrack, and have to focus in order to return to where we want to be, but as long as the will is there, and the wish sincere, we will find help (sometimes in the least expected of places or people.) There is also nothing wrong with

**SEE ALSO:**

Embracing Nature, pp. 84–87

Month Four: Time for Action, pp. 140–141

seeking help from the more experienced, especially when it comes to physical or mental health. Sometimes we simply can't do everything ourselves, even if that is our ultimate objective.

Humans can survive in most environments—sometimes even without technological help—but would you want to exist in an overpopulated world where everyone had to fight for every scrap of unhealthy food, every drop of polluted water, and every breath of tainted air? Can that be called life?

Remember, the planet can survive—and thrive—without us, but we can't exist without her. It's in our own best interests to ensure her health. We have a responsibility to care for everything that makes her—air, earth, and water, all the flora and fauna, and each other. Use the Craft to help make it happen.

# SACRED SPACES

**Sacred spaces are places consciously set apart from our usual day-to-day life where we can go to seek sanctuary and feel safe, commune with our deities, purify ourselves, and work to transform our lives.**

Churches, mosques, and temples are sacred spaces—but so are Uluru in Australia, Mount Fuji in Japan, Stonehenge in the UK, the Sacred Mountains in China, rivers—especially the Ganges, in India—the sweat lodges of indigenous Americans, the Mayan Cenote Sagrado in Mexico, the Devil's Tower in the US, and many, many more. There is a sacred space for everyone in the world, even if they don't necessarily recognize it as such. The professor's study, the scientist's lab, the astronomer's observatory, the green witch's garden, the kitchen witch's kitchen, the library for the academic, the source of life-changing knowledge, the teen's private bedroom, the womb within which the unborn baby grows in safety and security—all are examples of sacred spaces.

## CREATING A SACRED SPACE

Sacred spaces are what we make them. They do not need to be places of worship, unless we wish to make them so. They don't need to take a specific form, unless we wish them to—or unless to do so makes them symbolic of their purpose. Most churches look similar and perform similar functions, to be a place where humans can worship their gods and receive instruction from them. They can be under the open sky, in a sacred grove or circle, or in a structure such as a cave, tent, or building. Anywhere we can sit or stand or dance, in silence or in song, and feel the separateness and sanctity of the space is suitable.

**SEE ALSO:**

Your Sacred Space, pp. 88–89

Month One: Preparation, pp. 134–135

A sacred space serves a variety of purposes. No violence should take place within it, so it can be a useful place for airing grievances and turning arguments into debates. The nature of the space allows time to think before we speak and listen to and understand others' points of view. It's a calm, quiet place for meditation on ourselves, our responsibilities, and gifts, for asking for the blessings of whichever god or goddess we may revere, or for determining how we want to deal with any problems in our lives—if only to vow to return for a respite from the troubles of daily life.

Our personal sacred space should be comfortable for us, with cushions or appropriate seating, and lighting that we find calming and restful. If indoors, it can be decorated with things we find beautiful or inspiring. If outdoors, with fragrant or beautiful plants. Music can be quiet and gentle, or natural—birdsong and breeze. Everyone's idea of the perfect space is different, and may change over time.

Ultimately, the human body can be a sacred place, a vessel for silent communication with itself and with the forces that control life, a powerful force for transformation and change.

# THE SACRED CIRCLE

**The circle has been used for millennia, all across the globe, by all peoples. It's a symbol of unity and infinity. It symbolizes wholeness, totality, the all-encompassing universe, and the zero from which all things arise.**

The circle—and its three-dimensional extension, the sphere, orb, or globe, created in nature by gravity—is one of the most basic shapes in nature. We see planets, moons, the sun, and other stars as circles. It's the shape of mammalian eyes, of finger rings, of a full womb, of drops of water, of most fruits. It's a shape we associate with safety and normality.

A circle creates an enclosure. Inside is limited space, with restricted movement, bounded by the circle itself. Outside is unlimited space, wild and untamed, full of the unknown. A circle can be used as a safe place for protection against the evil energies outside it. A circle has no beginning and no end, making it symbolic of the cycles of nature and of the life-death-rebirth traditions of the Wise.

Sacred circles can represent many things: sanctuary, protection, a focus for power, a terrestrial astronomical observatory such as, possibly, Stonehenge, and a space dedicated to a particular function. Although they may share the same purposes as sacred spaces, they are deliberately designed and shaped for the creators' objectives and they are—as the name says and unlike most sacred spaces—actually circular.

**SEE ALSO:**

Your Sacred Space, pp. 88–89

Month One: Preparation, pp. 134–135

## CREATING A SACRED CIRCLE

The creation of a sacred circle is a deliberate, planned act. A particular need arises—perhaps a place where organized rituals can be held. The location is chosen for its specific significance—it may be at the junction of two ley lines, for example, or close to something that has been an object of reverence throughout history. Somewhere where it won't be easily discovered is best, simply to keep it private and unspoiled. The circle is constructed—from stones (upright or simply laid flat on the ground), wood, a circular line engraved or dug from the earth, salt (for purification), plants, or bushes—whatever the creators believe will serve their purpose best. An opening is made, usually facing a specific direction: midsummer sunrise, perhaps, for magic or rituals designed to work best in the summer, or midwinter sunrise, for winter rituals and ceremonies. Practitioners enter and leave through this opening without disturbing the outer line of the encompassing circle.

When the time is right—at the aforementioned solstices, for example—participants will gather while the circle is dedicated in a specially created ceremony. At this point its purpose is set, and from here on it will be used specifically for that reason. The work involved in creating and dedicating the circle help ensure its purpose in the minds and hearts of those who will use it, and even if outsiders—not realizing what it is—find and enter it, its purpose will remain clear and set.

# TOOLS OF THE CRAFT

**Several tools feature in the practice of Wicca and witchcraft, especially in traditional, initiatory or ceremonial practices.**

## BOOK OF SHADOWS

Popularized in the 1970s by Gardnerian Wicca, this was originally a book containing the spells, rites, and rituals used in the tradition. At one time there was only one Book of Shadows for each coven, held by the High Priest or High Priestess; these days every witch or Wiccan can—and should—create their own.

Your own Book of Shadows is, essentially, a journal of your experiences along the Path you have chosen (or that has chosen you). It may contain enlightening occurrences or inspirations, your own discoveries, details of things you have enjoyed and want to do again, personally important people you have met, new things you have tried and how they made you feel, salutations to your chosen deities, rituals you have performed, and spells you have tried and how they have worked.

Your book should be completely private and can take any form you want: an actual paper and ink book, a typed folder of thoughts, a video diary, a series of drawings, or a mix of all of them. It can be as large or small as you like, plain or decorative. It can be handwritten in your native language, any language you know, or even in a language or code you create especially for it. You can make a daily, weekly, or monthly ritual of adding to it, though it should be updated as soon as you have something you want to add, rather than waiting, as you may forget details.

You are free to create a Book of Shadows that best represents yourself, and dedicate it to that purpose. If you do choose to create one, be sure to use it when needed, and not just hide it away and forget about it. The book should eventually feel like a part of you.

**SEE ALSO:**

Choosing Your Tools, pp. 90–91

Month One: Preparation, pp. 134–135

## ALTAR

It is very important to have somewhere to practice your craft and keep your tools safe, and it can be as private or as obvious as you like! An altar is the traditional tool: a small table, perhaps with a drawer for your smaller tools, that you don't use for anything else.

Alternatives are an outdoor altar—maybe a flat stone supported by three stone "legs," or a small wooden table hidden away in a copse or behind a bush, or even a birdtable or birdbath.

You could even dedicate a space in a conservatory or a greenhouse, which has the added benefit of being sheltered from unpleasant weather while still being "outside."

# ELEMENTAL TOOLS

**The traditional elemental tools are the wand, athame, chalice, and pentacle—they represent the natural elements.**

## THE WAND

Wands represent the element of air externally, and intellect internally. They can be made of wood, metal, a long quartz crystal—anything that lends itself to the basic shape. They can also be any length, though for practicality's sake 9–12in (23–30cm) is probably the best. A wand is used symbolically to channel your intellect into solving problems and bringing enlightenment.

## THE ATHAME

An athame, or ceremonial knife, represents fire externally, and willpower internally. Traditionally the athame was made of metal and had a black handle. Today, for legal and health purposes it's safest to use something relatively blunt, like a paperknife. Its traditional use was to direct energy—when casting spells or drawing a magic circle, for example. These days it symbolizes willpower "cutting through" problems or encouraging determination to achieve your aims.

## THE CHALICE

Chalices represent water externally, and emotion internally. In some traditions they symbolize the womb of the Threefold Goddess (see page 48) and her gift of bringing forth life. A chalice can be as large as a cauldron or as small as a wine glass, and made from any material. Filled with water, it can be used as a scrying mirror. Filled with wine it's a celebration of fertility and the good things in life.

**See also:**

Choosing Your Tools, pp. 92–93

Month One: Preparation, pp. 134–135

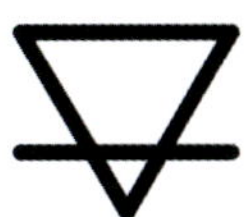

### THE PENTACLE

The pentacle—a disk of stone, crystal, or metal—represents the element of earth externally, and strength and common sense internally. Traditionally the pentacle was inscribed with arcane protective symbols to sanctify the altar. Today it can be used as a symbol of our grounding in the earth of the world that gave us birth.

## RITUAL CLOTHES

Some practitioners devote a specific outfit or robe to wear when performing rituals. This is not absolutely necessary, but it can make the occasion feel more meaningful. If you choose to do so, it should be something made of natural fabric, loose, comfortable, and fairly hardwearing as you may be using it for some years. It doesn't need a dedication, unless you wish to do so, as simply wearing it for every occasion gives it purpose and ceremonial meaning.

## THE FAMILIAR

The word "familiar" originally referred to supernatural entities who served a witch, obeyed her commands, and generally looked after her. They could be deadly to anyone who injured or threatened their witch. They usually took the form of a familiar creature to avoid suspicion, and since the witch or wise woman throughout history has kept a pet—very often a cat for their independence and usefulness in keeping down the number of rodents—the animal was viewed (often unfavorably) as her familiar spirit.

Cats were the most frequent familiars, especially black cats, which led most unfairly and wrongly to them being viewed as unlucky. A black cat is much the same as any other cat—just not so easy to see at night.

Felines still make very popular pets these days. They are relatively easy to look after, and capable of showing a great deal of love. You don't need to deem your cat a familiar spirit, but by owning one you are carrying on a centuries-old tradition.

If keeping a cat isn't possible, consider adopting a wild native creature as a familiar. It's very unlikely you'll be able to make a pet of it, but the traditional qualities of the animal can be very enlightening. Consider the magical fox, the survivor, set in the sky as the constellation Vulpecula; the resourceful tool-making crow, high above us in the constellation of Corvus; or the playful, intelligent dolphin, leaping in the heavens in the stars of Delphinus.

**SEE ALSO:**

Choosing Your Tools, pp. 90–93

Month One: Preparation, pp. 134–135

## BROOMSTICKS

A ceremonial besom or broom symbolizes a cleansing of the sacred space, "sweeping clean" the area in which to conduct rituals or cast spells. The image of the witch riding on a broomstick was taken from this practice.

A broom was also, in some traditions, jumped over when handfasting (originally a Wiccan, neopagan "marriage" that entered the mainstream for alternative wedding ceremonies in the 2000s). Handfasting is an unofficial wedding, sometimes with the intent of performing a second, officially binding wedding later, or a binding betrothal. Originally simply a firm clasping of the couple's hands, at some point—possibly influenced by other countries' traditions—the hands were wrapped with a rope or ribbon to express the binding nature of the contract. Hence "tying the knot" to mean marriage in modern idiom.

# ELEMENTAL MAGIC

**The natural world and its magic are less about physical treasure and more about inner riches.**

Traditionally, Western elemental magic was magic performed by the control of the four original, basic elements of air, fire, earth, and water, and by the fifth, superior element, the human spirit. In China the elements are wood, fire, earth, metal, and water, while in Japan they are earth, water, fire, wind, and void. We'll only consider the Western aspects here.

To work magic of any kind requires a few basics—a need for something or a goal to reach, the ability to focus tightly to visualize receiving the thing desired, or achieving that goal, and a clear understanding of what it will mean to you. Each magic activity is closed with a spell or incantation for success.

With elemental magic, the simpler the process, the more likely it is to have the result you want. You may perform a spell for treasure, and it's always possible you'll win the lottery or be left a large inheritance, but it's more likely you'll find riches in your family, friends, and loved ones, or in a deeper and surprisingly profitable new insight or flash of intuition.

Create your own ritual, ceremony, and incantation. Use what you find here as a guide. It's your own passion, need, belief, and dedication that will work the magic.

**SEE ALSO:**

Calling on the Elements, pp. 94–95

## AIR

Air is represented by the wand externally, and symbolizes the intellect and understanding. Traditionally its color is yellow and white, its direction east, and its season spring. Incense is a specialty for air magic, and incantations and meditations for healing and cleansing of body, mind, and spirit. Yellow and white crystals are appropriate for air magic. If you wish to use cards, in the tarot the wands suite, and in playing cards the clubs suite, are the ones to employ.

## FIRE

Fire is represented by the athame externally, and symbolizes the will and determination. Traditionally its colors are red and gold, and it's associated with the south and summer. Candles are best for fire magic, which may involve creativity, passion, and power. Red and gold crystals are suitable for fire magic. If you wish to use cards, in the tarot the swords suite, and in playing cards the spades suite, are the ones to employ.

## WATER

Water is represented by the chalice externally, and symbolizes the emotions and instinct. Traditionally its colors are blue and silver, its direction west, and its season fall. Chalices and bowls of water are most effective here, for peace, divination, and dreams. Blue and silver crystals are the best for water magic. If you wish to use cards, in the tarot the cups suite, and in playing cards the hearts suite, are the ones to employ.

## EARTH

Earth is represented by the pentacle externally, and symbolizes strength and common sense. Traditionally its colors are green and copper-brown, its direction north, and its season winter. Crystals, especially green and brown stones, and salt are effective in earth magic, which is usually concerned with wealth, good luck, and fertility. Wood and small pieces of metal are suitable also. If you wish to use cards, in the tarot the pentacles suite, and in playing cards the diamonds suite, are the ones to employ.

## SPIRIT

There is no traditional symbol for spirit, but it has occasionally been represented by the figure of a human superimposed onto a pentacle or a pentacle in a circle. Its essence is control and manipulation—the ability to use the other elements wisely and constructively. Spirit magic is usually performed silently, without any outward symbols, tools, or panoply. It's performed within our own minds, when we are alone and quiet and can listen to what our heart and mind are telling us. It can cause life-changing transformations of behavior from self-destructive to positive and vitally constructive, or as simple as realizing how much someone means to us, and how we can show them our love.

## A BLESSING FOR CHANGE

To be said before preparing to work elemental magic.

**"Mother Earth, great Goddess and great God, spirits of the elements, hear me,**
**Grant me the insight and power to make the changes, small or great,**
**To be the person I truly want to be.**
**Bless my endeavors and empower me with your Wisdom,**
**And let me honor you in everything I do.**
**So might it be."**

**SEE ALSO:**

Elemental Tools, pp. 34–35

Calling on the Elements, pp. 94–95

# THE MAGIC OF COLOR

Color has a role to play in witchcraft; it can be used symbolically to represent natural elements, festivals, and seasons, but also to create moods that influence our emotions.

The light that we can see occupies quite a narrow band within the electromagnetic spectrum, between the infrared and the ultraviolet (outside of this band are very low-frequency radio waves and microwaves at the red end and X-rays and gamma rays at the violet end). Light from the sun appears white, but is actually made up of a rainbow of wavelengths of colors that we can see if we direct sunlight through a prism. The colors of the objects we see are determined by which wavelengths of light the object reflects.

That being said, color has its own magic. We respond physically, mentally, and emotionally to different colors, depending on their innate symbolism and how and when they are used. There are a vast number of shades and hues between the primary colors listed here, and to some extent they will share the effects of the main color comprising them.

**SEE ALSO:**

Working With Color, pp. 96–97

## THE MAGIC OF COLOR

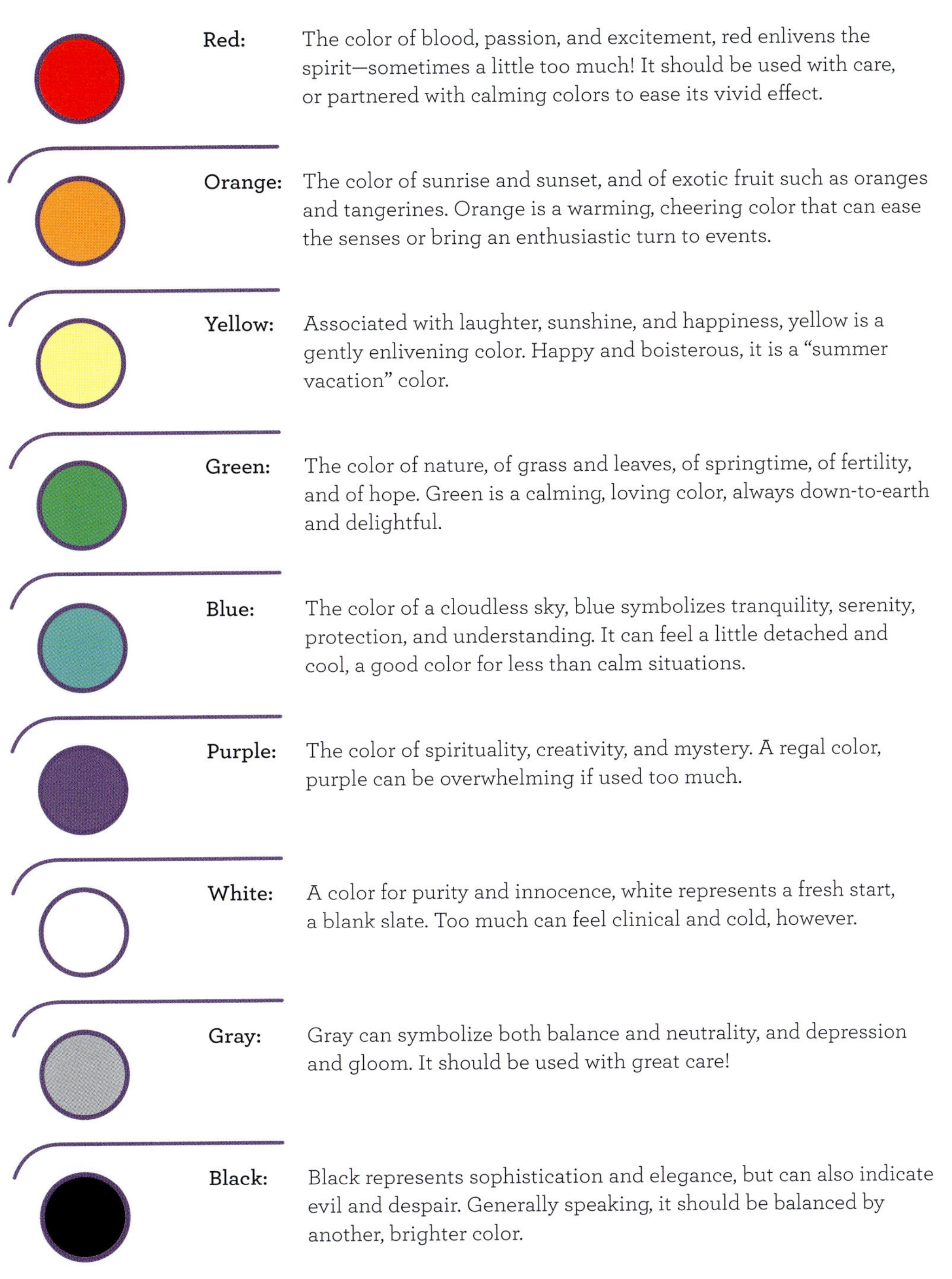

**Red:** The color of blood, passion, and excitement, red enlivens the spirit—sometimes a little too much! It should be used with care, or partnered with calming colors to ease its vivid effect.

**Orange:** The color of sunrise and sunset, and of exotic fruit such as oranges and tangerines. Orange is a warming, cheering color that can ease the senses or bring an enthusiastic turn to events.

**Yellow:** Associated with laughter, sunshine, and happiness, yellow is a gently enlivening color. Happy and boisterous, it is a "summer vacation" color.

**Green:** The color of nature, of grass and leaves, of springtime, of fertility, and of hope. Green is a calming, loving color, always down-to-earth and delightful.

**Blue:** The color of a cloudless sky, blue symbolizes tranquility, serenity, protection, and understanding. It can feel a little detached and cool, a good color for less than calm situations.

**Purple:** The color of spirituality, creativity, and mystery. A regal color, purple can be overwhelming if used too much.

**White:** A color for purity and innocence, white represents a fresh start, a blank slate. Too much can feel clinical and cold, however.

**Gray:** Gray can symbolize both balance and neutrality, and depression and gloom. It should be used with great care!

**Black:** Black represents sophistication and elegance, but can also indicate evil and despair. Generally speaking, it should be balanced by another, brighter color.

# THE MAGIC OF HERBS

Discover traditional uses for herbs in the Craft, for both physical and magical purposes.

**A number of herbs have traditional associations with certain deities, and also with medical practices. It's old knowledge, for example, that one of the original painkillers was willowbark, which contains salicylic acid, a primary ingredient in aspirin, and that the digitalis used in heart medications came from foxgloves.**

Placed on the altar, either fresh or dried, herbs may use their traditional magic to empower spells and salutations. Fresh sunflowers make excellent accompaniments to salutations to the Sun God, for example, and may aid spells for fertility, while the empty silver seedpods of honesty are perfect for greetings to the Moon Goddess in any of her phases. They may also prove effective in spells for wealth, and for fending off nightmares. Herbal or floral fragrances are effective in reed diffusers, and may be preferable to incense sticks, which produce smoke and may cause a fire risk.

Herbs and flowers that traditionally repel nightmares and aid peaceful sleep can be placed, fresh, in a vase at the head of the bed, or, dried, added to pillows to release their fragrances during sleep. Handmade sachets containing herbs for protection, healing, or prosperity can be carried in a pocket or bag to attract the desired aim to the carrier. For extra power they should be made by the person who will carry them, and closed up with a spell for effectiveness.

## HERBS TO USE

Here are some traditional herbs and their physical and magical uses. Note that the correspondences are traditional only and should not be taken as proven cures. There's no harm in trying them for their magical qualities, however, as long as you carry them. Don't consume anything on this list, unless you know it is safe. If this is the case, and you wish to try them to help ease minor ailments, bless the plant and ask for its help before using.

**SEE ALSO:**

Ways with Herbs, pp. 98–99

## THE MAGIC OF HERBS

| HERB | MEDICINAL USES | MAGICAL USES |
|---|---|---|
| Angelica | Helps ease colic and stomach pains | Protects the house and garden |
| Basil | Good for fevers and the stomach | Banishes negativity and attracts love |
| Camomile | Good for insomnia | Attracts money, used in purifying rituals |
| Chives | Aids healthy bones | Fends off evil spirits |
| Cloves | Good for colds and congestion | Attracts prosperity and good luck |
| Comfrey | Good for broken bones and wounds | Protects the traveler |
| Daisy | Good for headaches | Brings good luck |
| Garlic | Natural antibiotic | Guards the house, dispels negativity |
| Ginger | Stimulates the immune system | Speeds up the coming to fruition of personal plans |
| Heather | Suppresses coughs and aids sleep | Guards against violent crime |
| Lavender | Antidepressant and relaxant | Used for healing of body, mind, and spirit |
| Lemon Balm | Eases stings, headaches, colds | Used in spells for friendship, healing |
| Marjoram | Helps ease asthma and coughs | Eases grief |
| Oregano | Helps ease allergies and infections | Aids happiness, health, and letting go |
| Parsley | Strengthens bones, helps eyesight | Promotes fertility and happiness |
| Patchouli (plant) | Helps ease diarrhea and nausea | Defends against evil |
| Peppermint | Used for colds, fevers, nausea, relaxation and stress reduction | Used for healing and mental clarity |
| Rose | Nourishes the skin | Used in love spells |
| Rosemary | Improves memory and recognition | Deflects evil |
| Sage | Eases sore throats and stomach pains | Banishes evil and aids purification |
| Thyme | Used as an antiseptic | Repels nightmares |
| Turmeric | Used as a mood stabilizer | Protects and purifies |
| Valerian | Aids restful sleep | Helps couples make up after rows |
| Yarrow | Eases toothache | Wards off fear and negativity |

# THE MAGIC OF OILS

Discover traditional uses for oils in the Craft, for magical purposes.

**Oil of one sort or another is everywhere, from the oils in our skin to the oils that keep the wheels and engines of industry turning. Generally, though, we're mainly concerned with oils for massage and other physical aspects, for rituals and anointing, for use as perfumes, and in fragrancers. Only a drop or two is needed for any function, and none of these oils should be consumed.**

Ritual oils are used to anoint candles, the altar, the tools, and—if made safely and properly—the body in preparation for a ceremony or ritual. Such oils are usually stored in special, ritually blessed vessels. While it is possible to extract pure oil from many herbs yourself, it is usually a very time- and labor-intensive process. Ready-prepared oils are more usual.

Before use, anointing oil should be blessed with a spell for its purpose, be it for health or as a token of consecration to the Craft. A drop of the oil can then be placed on candles and tools on the altar, to consecrate them to their purpose. A drop or two may also be placed on the forehead of those taking part in the ritual or celebration.

Fragranced oils can be used sparingly as personal perfumes. The more exotic fragrances—ylang-ylang, jasmine, patchouli—as well as the more Western traditional perfumes such as rose and gardenia, may be used both in rituals and on the body when working personal or sex magic. Much depends on choice. Whatever the purpose, a quick spell or blessing before use may increase the potency of an oil's effect.

**SEE ALSO:**

Ways with Oils, pp. 100–101

## OILS TO USE

Here are some traditional oils and their magical uses. Note that the correspondences are traditional only and should not be taken as proven cures. As with herbs, there is no harm in trying these oils for their magical qualities, but do not consume anything on this list.

| OIL | MAGICAL USES |
|---|---|
| Basil | Stimulates the mind and imagination and encourages peace between individuals |
| Bergamot | Used in rituals concerning money and protection |
| Camphor | For purification, and to promote celibacy |
| Cedarwood | To enhance spirituality |
| Cypress | To help ease the loss of loved ones, and for blessings and protection |
| Eucalyptus | For purification and healing |
| Frankincense | To aid mediation, especially on spiritual matters |
| Grapefruit | To purify and enliven |
| Jasmine | Promotes love, peace, and psychic awareness |
| Juniper | For protection and moon ceremonies |
| Lemongrass | To lift the spirit and sharpen the mind |
| Myrrh | To aid meditation and assist emotional healing |
| Pine | For purification, healing, and protection |
| Sandalwood | For meditation, and for sexual matters |
| Ylang-ylang | To encourage gentle love and loving sex |

# DEITIES OF THE CRAFT

**Craft deities, the Threefold Goddess, the Horned God, and the Green Man symbolize birth, change, death, and rebirth, representing wholeness, the cycle of the Earth, and the passing of time.**

## THE THREEFOLD GODDESS

The tradition of the Threefold Goddess is very ancient. Symbolizing the three major aspects, or archetypes, of the female, they appear in many faiths and forms.

In Greek tradition they are the three Graces: Aglaea (Shining), Euphrosyne (Joy), and Thalia (Blooming). They are also represented by the three goddesses of Fate: Clotho, Lachesis, and Atropos, collectively known as the Moirai (pictured below), whose duty it is to ensure that every being lives out their lives according to the laws of the universe.

In Roman mythology the Fates are the Parcae, or Destinies: Nona, who spins the thread of life; Decima, who measures the thread of life; and Morta, who chooses the manner of a being's death and cuts the thread of life accordingly.

Mœræ, or the Fates.

**SEE ALSO:**

Honor Your Deities, pp. 102–105

In India the archetypes are the Tridevi: Saraswati (goddess of learning, cosmic intelligence, knowledge, and consciousness); Lakshmi (goddess of wealth, fertility, fulfillment, exaltation, and magnificence); and Parvati (goddess of war, love and beauty).

In Japan the archetypes are Benzaiten (goddess of everything that flows—water, music, time, speech, and knowledge), Kisshoten (goddess of beauty, happiness, and fertility), and Daikokuten (deity of fortune, agriculture, the household, and war).

The Celts saw her as representing the nature of the universe as a whole, much of which is unknown and unknowable (before birth and after death, and what happens before rebirth). For example, Brigid, goddess of poetry, agriculture, and healing, was seen as three sisters: one reigning over all forms of verse; one symbolizing agriculture and blacksmithing; and one concerned with healing and the particular care of women.

## MAIDEN, MOTHER, CRONE

In the Craft, the Threefold Goddess is seen as having many forms and as many different names, but the tendency is to view her as Maiden, Mother, and Crone, representing the three main stages of female life: the Maiden as child, full of enthusiasm and potential, the Mother, maternal, loving, and the carrier of the future, and the Crone, filled with the wisdom that comes from a full life well lived. They are symbolized by the three phases of the moon—waxing crescent (Maiden), full moon (Mother), waning crescent (Crone).

She has multiple images, functions, and names. In the English-based language alone she is Anu, Brigid, Ceridwen, Diana, Danu, Hecate, Isis, Morigan, Selene, and more. We are not restricted to celebrating, worshipping, or developing a spiritual relationship with just one aspect—"Thou shalt have no other gods before me" has no place in the Craft.

## THE HORNED GOD

As ancient a deity as the Threefold Goddess, the Horned God is her consort, and the god of nature, fertility, sexuality, wildness, and hunting. He goes by a variety of names: Atho, Bran, Cernnunos, Herne the Hunter, Karnayna, Pan, Pashupati. He is visualized as having two horns, or antlers, to represent his wild, dual nature. The two symbolize opposites: night and day, summer and winter, light and dark. He is occasionally depicted as having cloven hooves and the legs of a goat or deer.

The Oak King of the Light Half of the year (spring, summer) symbolizes one aspect, while the Holly King of the Dark Half of the year (fall, winter) represents the other. He can be as wild as a beast, and as kind and compassionate as a father.

In traditional Wicca, the god's dual nature combines with the goddess's threefold aspect to create the pentagram, which symbolizes the five elements (fire, air, earth, water, and spirit) that make up the human being. The god and the goddess are intimately intertwined in the natural world.

Unfortunately, the image of the Horned God was appropriated and made more bestial by the Christian religion to represent their devil. The god's sexuality became a dire thing in monotheistic religions, as well, and his equality with the goddess may well have led, through twisted patriarchal thinking, to the female being seen as less than the male, led purely by her "animalistic urges" instead of human consciousness, a perversion of nature—an image that still exists in some places today.

Truly, the Horned God is a passionate, joyful god in his own right, the personification of all the natural things of the world and a deep, exultant lust for life. His union with the goddess at the sabbat of Beltane is one of the most glorious representations of the joy of living, and is always to be celebrated!

**SEE ALSO:**

Honor Your Deities, pp. 102–105

## THE GREEN MAN

Represented as a male human face surrounded, made from, or occasionally partly obscured, by leaves and vines, the Green Man is primarily a symbol of the rebirth of green, growing things in spring. Originally a pagan symbol, the "foliate head" or "foliate mask"—as the image is generally known—nevertheless appears as carvings in many Christian institutions. It may be that this was a way to bridge the gap between pagan beliefs and the new Christian religion. There's nothing obviously sinister about a foliate head—in fact, it's usually quite a charming image.

The Green Man may be a representation of other deities such as Dionysus, Lud, Odin, Osiris, and may be associated with the character known as Jack in the Green in English folklore, celebrated at the sabbat of Beltane as a symbol of the festival's fertility and vitality. There is a tradition that Robin Hood was an incarnation of the Green Man; he gave generously to the poor, after all (although there's nothing to suggest that the Green Man stole from the rich in order to spread his bounty).

In some Wiccan traditions, the Green Man represents the Horned God in his spring rebirth aspect. However we view him, he is a joyful, cheerful symbol of spring!

# THE SABBATS

"Sabbat" is the generic name for each of the eight fire festivals of the year.

These eight festivals comprise four quarter days—the equinoxes and the solstices—and the four cross-quarter days—the festivals that come halfway between the quarter days.

## QUARTER DAYS

The equinox and solstice dates vary by a few days from year to year, depending on when the sun reaches its most northerly or southerly position. In the northern hemisphere, the dates are as follows:

- **Eostre** (pronounced EE-strah; the spring (vernal) equinox) falls around March 19–22
- **Litha** (the summer solstice) falls around June 19–23
- **Mabon** (the fall equinox) falls around September 21–24
- **Yule** (the winter solstice) falls around December 20–23

## CROSS-QUARTER DAYS

The cross-quarter days always start on the same date*.
In the northern hemisphere, the dates are as follows:

- **Imbolc** (pronounced IM-bolk): February 1–2
- **Beltane** (pronounced BEL-tane): May 1–2
- **Lughnasadh** (pronounced LOO-nus-suh): August 1–2
- **Samhain** (pronounced SOW-en): October 31–November 1

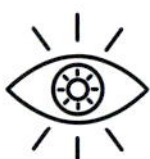

**SEE ALSO:**

Practicing Witchcraft, pp. 106–121

Your Witchcraft Year, pp. 132–133

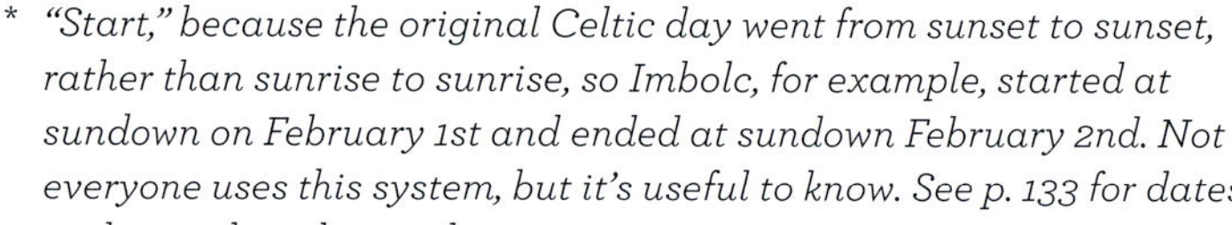

* *"Start," because the original Celtic day went from sunset to sunset, rather than sunrise to sunrise, so Imbolc, for example, started at sundown on February 1st and ended at sundown February 2nd. Not everyone uses this system, but it's useful to know. See p. 133 for dates in the southern hemisphere.*

## SABBAT SYMBOLISM

Farther back in time, the year was reputed to be divided into the Light Half (Beltane to Samhain) and the Dark Half (Samhain to Beltane). The Light Half was for planting and growing, and the Dark Half for harvesting and preparation for the coming year.

Each sabbat represented a different stage of the agricultural cycle, and by extension the stages of human life. They were celebrated with fire in one form or another—usually bonfires that were often danced around—and with feasts in which the whole community shared food, drink, merry-making, and singing.

Most of the festivals made their way into the modern world, usually appropriated by the Christian religion (it was, after all, easier to persuade people to adopt the new religious festivals if they resembled or replaced traditional ones—hence, Eostre became Easter and Yule became Christmas). Many of the symbols of the original festivals carried over into the Christian traditions: Easter rabbits (originally hares for the goddess Brigid) and eggs, Hallowe'en/All Soul's Day for Samhain, Christmas trees for Yule trees.

Today the fire festivals offer regular breaks from daily toil, and a chance to reconnect with friends and family, let loose, enjoy the day, and give thanks to whichever aspects of the god and goddess we feel closest to.

# IMBOLC

Cross-Quarter Day • Candlemas • February 1–2

**In the northern hemisphere, Imbolc marks the midway point between Yule and the spring equinox at Eostre. It lasts from the evening of February 1 to sundown on February 2 and celebrates the first stirrings of spring. It's the first cross-quarter day, the first fire festival, and the first sabbat of the year.**

Imbolc is the festival of the wise, powerful goddess Brigid ("the exalted one" in ancient Celtic lore, eventually Christianized as St. Brigid; also called Bride and Brigantia in other cultures). She represents the Maiden form of the Threefold Goddess, and is the goddess of healing, poetry, domesticated animals, blacksmithing, and the protector of women. As we've already noted, the goddess in all her forms is central and essential to the Craft. In her incarnation as Brigid she symbolizes rebirth and the growing fertility of spring.

Imbolc is a time of renewed energy and personal growth for the followers of the Craft. The etymology of the word is still uncertain, but may mean "in the womb" and refer to pregnant ewes, as Imbolc occurs before the lambing season, and was the herald of the season of giving birth for the domesticated animals that formed such a vital part of farming and feeding the nation.

**See also:**

Imbolc Activities, pp. 106–107

Month Two: Imbolc, pp. 136–137

## THE IMBOLC ALTAR

Imbolc is celebrated with the symbols of Brigid. The altar should be decorated with white and green: a white and green cloth, preferably depicting spring flowers, is appropriate. The traditional flower is the snowdrop. If possible, a small white or transparent vase filled with snowdrops should be set on the altar, along with a white candle and a bowl of milk.

Imbolc's trees are the rowan and the willow. Small branches of these are ideal to place on, or before, the altar (depending on their size). The willow is very flexible, and symbolizes movement and transformation—"bending, not breaking"—which is emblematic of the upwelling energy and power of spring. The rowan holds a special place in Celtic and Wiccan legend. It's the tree of life and protection, representing women, motherhood, birth, and survival. It's capable of growing and thriving in the most inhospitable of places, and is considered one of the "pioneering" species of plants, the first to move into a barren environment.

## CELEBRATING IMBOLC

Today the fire festivals offer regular breaks from daily toil, and a chance to reconnect with friends and family, let loose, enjoy the day, and give thanks to whichever aspects of the god and goddess you feel closest to. A blessing for spring should be said, and simple food—bread and cheese (ewe's milk cheese if possible)—shared with friends at the closing of the ceremony. Blackberries are considered to be special to Brigid, so to complete the celebration of her festival, drink blackberry wine or juice.

# EOSTRE

Quarter Day • Spring Equinox • March 19–22
Alternatively called Ostara and purloined as Easter in the Christian tradition

**Eostre is the goddess of the dawn, and her festival celebrates the fullness and blossoming of spring and the season of seed sowing for the crops that will be harvested in the fall. It's the season of brightly blooming flowers, and the appearance of the hares that are a symbol of the goddess and fertility.**

The festival symbolizes abundance, new life, and balance, as represented by being the point in the spring when the day and night are of equal length. Eostre is the first cross-quarter day, second fire festival, and second sabbat of the year. (The cross-quarter days can vary by a couple of days each year, depending on solar and lunar placements.)

Eggs are a primary symbol of this festival. They represent mystery, huge potential, and the beginnings of life. Around this festival the weather starts growing warmer, and birds start laying their eggs after the cold and darkness of the winter. The brimstone butterfly—the first butterfly of the year—is a big, brilliant yellow-green flash of sunshine dedicated to the goddess of the dawn. It lays its eggs on buckthorn, one of the earlier flowering trees of the year, and the caterpillars feed on the leaves. The adult butterflies prefer the nectar of purplish blue flowers, and have a particular liking for bluebells.

**SEE ALSO:**

Eostre Activities, pp. 108–109

Month Three: Eostre, pp. 138–139

## THE EOSTRE ALTAR

The altar should be decorated in green, pink, and yellow, with pink and/or yellow candles, a small dish of honey, a small dish of seeds, and honeysuckle branches. Add pink, white, and yellow flowers, preferably wildflowers (daffodils, primroses, yellow or pink crocuses, celandine); acorns, for growth and wisdom; eggs, for infinite potential; and fresh fruit, for the taste of the coming summer.

Eostre's trees are the slender, dancing birch, from which the brooms to sweep away the old were traditionally made, and the ash, represented by Yggdrasil, the cosmic tree that linked the world of humanity with the spiritual realm, symbolizing the interconnectedness of all things.

## CELEBRATING EOSTRE

Celebrate the festival with friends or partners, love, laughter, and song. It's a joyous time. End the celebration with honeycakes, or simple toast with butter and honey, and mead. You can drink honey dissolved in hot water instead. If the weather is willing, go out to watch the sunset.

# BELTANE

Cross-Quarter Day • May Day • May 1

**Beltane is May Day, the third of the sabbats and fire festivals and the second cross-quarter day of the year, midway between spring and summer. Traditionally set when the May tree—the hawthorn—first blossoms and marking the first signs of summer, Beltane is a celebration brimming over with life, vitality, passion, and fertility. It is the start of the growing season in all senses of the word.**

The name comes from the Celtic *bel*, "the bright one" and *teine* "fire." It is the festival of the "goodly fire," and originally bonfires were lit to honor the sun—bonfires whose smoke and ashes had special protective powers. People would lead their cattle between the fires to grant them protection for the year, and the household fires were doused and relit from the Beltane fires. The fit and healthy were known to "jump the fire," literally leaping over the flames once they had died down a little, to prove their virility and fitness to have children.

Beltane marks one of the two times of year when the veil between the worlds of the living and the realm of the dead are thinnest, and communication could, if one was lucky, pass between the worlds. (The other is Samhain, modern-day Halloween.)

## THE BELTANE ALTAR

The colors of Beltane are green, red, and white and these should be used to cover the altar as well as being worn by festivalgoers. Hawthorn branches are seen as charms for the greatest good luck. The altar should be decorated with these, as well as flowers, ribbons, and seashells. People also decorate the doors and windows of their homes.

**SEE ALSO:**

Beltane Activities, pp. 110–111

Month Five: Beltane, pp. 142–143

## CELEBRATING BELTANE

Traditionally Beltane was a time for handfastings—weddings that, in some traditions, lasted a year and a day—and great feasts. It is a time of fertility and sexuality, when the young of many species, including humans, are conceived. This was also the time when the Green Man married the May Queen. The dew collected on Beltane morning is reputed to preserve youth and bestow beauty on the person who washes their face in it. Holy wells are visited and offerings for health, fertility, and virility left there.

Today, the festival is often celebrated by dancing around a maypole, which represents fertility and the creation of life, and the transition from lust to love and commitment.

Bread and oatmeal, wine and strawberries are eaten and drunk to celebrate the festival with love and laughter, and old enmities are forgotten.

# LITHA

Quarter Day • Summer Solstice • June 19–23

**The height of summer, the longest day and shortest night of the year, the great fire festival of achievement and fulfillment—Litha is a glorious time of year. The origin of the name is debateable. It may come from the Anglo-Saxon for "June" or it may mean "gentle"—either are appropriate for the nature of the festival.**

Bel the sun god is at his most powerful and bountiful now, and is fêted in the figure of the wise, benevolent Oak King. The Maiden Goddess is about to become the Mother Goddess, nurturing, maternal, and beloved. Everything in nature celebrates the joy of being alive.

An ancient tradition in the UK and parts of Europe was to tie straw around and over a cartwheel until it was completely covered, set fire to it, and roll it down a hill to a river or stream. If the fire wheel reached the water and was put out, the harvests would be abundant and all hopes and wishes would come true. If it didn't get that far, the harvest wouldn't be so abundant, and people's wishes would be disappointed.

## THE LITHA ALTAR

The colors for Litha are blue for the summer sky, green for the grass and the leaves, and all the riotous colors of summer flowers. The altar should be covered with flowers, herbs, and oak leaves. Yellow and green candles should stand on the altar, too. The elder tree is symbolic of renewal, transformation, and change, and with the oak tree representing strength, endurance, and courage the two trees encompass all the virtues of the festival.

**SEE ALSO:**

Litha Activities, pp. 112–113

Month Six: Litha, pp. 144–145

## CELEBRATING LITHA

Medicinal herbs are at their most effective at Litha, and can be picked and prepared for use during the coming winter. This is also a good time to gather flowers for wine-making—roses and elderflowers, in particular, are at their fullest. Gather wildflowers and herbs to exchange as gifts between friends.

It is traditional to stay up all night on Midsummer's Eve, to dance around a bonfire lit on the top of a hill or near a holy well, and to watch and welcome the sunrise on Midsummer's Day. Returning home, feasts and dancing fill the day, with friends and neighbors in cheerful harmony.

# LUGHNASADH

Cross-Quarter Day • Lammas • Aug 1–2

**Lughnasadh is "the gathering of Lugh," the warrior sun god, the living spirit of the grain who brings in the harvest. This is the third cross-quarter day of the year, and, in some traditions, the festival of the First Fruits of the Harvest. Lammas comes from the Anglo-Saxon for "loaf-mass," "mass" most probably meaning "assembly" or "meeting." The name of the festival generally implies "the celebration of the grain that makes the bread that feeds us."**

Traditionally, at Lughnasadh, the sun god of the harvest sacrifices himself to the Threefold Goddess in her aspect as the Earth Mother, and his blood spills on the land to fertilize it for next year's crops. It sounds grim, but it is a willing, happy sacrifice that ensures the fruitfulness of the land and the continuation of life and should be celebrated as such.

## THE LUGHNASADH ALTAR

A Lughnasadh altar should be decorated in green and all shades of gold, from yellow to the deepest orange. Candles should be green and orange, and fruit scented if possible. Flowers should include meadowsweet, if available, and marigolds, sage leaves, mint, cornstalks (in the form of a corn dolly), and seeds—sunflower, mustard, and sesame seeds are readily available.

Hazel is the tree most associated with Lughnasadh. It is reputed to provide wisdom and inspiration. The Celts believed that hazelnuts fed the salmon and made it the wisest of fish. Whether you can glean wisdom from eating the fish is debatable, but they are indeed delicious, and a good choice for a Lughnasadh feast when served with freshly made bread. Hazel also, symbolically,

**SEE ALSO:**

Lughnasadh Activities, pp. 114–115

Month Eight: Lughnasadh, pp. 148–149

provided protection from venomous snakes and poisonous creeping things—scorpions and insects—if placed near or on the door of your house.

Prickly, protective gorse is another plant associated with this festival. It was traditionally believed never to stop flowering—hence the old saying, "Kissing's out of fashion when the gorse is out of blossom." It's not quite true, but gorse does have a very long flowering season, and makes excellent cover for small birds and animals. It's a lucky plant to have growing in the garden.

## CELEBRATING LUGHNASADH

As with all fire festivals, bonfires are lit and circles danced gladly around them. The first sheaf of grain—wheat, oats, barley, rye, whatever the farmer has grown and was ready for harvest—is cut and a loaf made from it, to be shared amongst friends and family.

Seed is a principal concept of Lughnasadh—the seed that contains within it all the future generations of grain, and in human terms, the ovum, which contains the potential for all future generations of humans. It has near-mystical properties, and is reverenced during this festival.

# MABON

Quarter Day • Fall equinox • September 21–24

**Named for the Welsh god Mabon (pronunced MAY-bon in English and MAH-bon in Welsh), who is the Child of Light, son of the Earth Mother. The name was first brought into use for the festival in 1970. Prior to that, it was simply known as Harvest Home. This is the second of the three harvests—the Harvest of Fruits—and a time of thanksgiving and celebration. It is also a time to rest from the labors of the harvest and prepare for the coming Dark Half of the year.**

Mabon marks the year's great Thanksgiving Feast. The day and night are again of equal length, and the year is in balance. The last of the grain has been reaped, the god of the grain harvest has now given his all to ensure bountiful crops for next year, and the first of the winter vegetables, fruits, and berries are now gathered. The usual bonfires are lit, people dance and sing, feast and drink, although perhaps in a more leisurely, calmer manner than the previous festivals.

The apple is the symbol of Mabon, representing everything good—health, life, immortality, healing, wholeness, regeneration, renewed beauty, youth, and long life.

## THE MABON ALTAR

The colors of Mabon are the colors of fall—reds, browns, yellows, oranges, golds, the hues of fall leaves and rose-red apples. Altars should be decorated with fruits of all kinds, along with rosehips, elderberries, and blackberries, red or golden candles, and a small bowl of beer or wine. A small offering—flowers, fruits, nuts, and berries—could be left out as a token gift for the nature spirits who have guarded and guided the harvest that we can now enjoy over the coming months.

**SEE ALSO:**

Mabon Activities, pp. 116–117

Month Nine: Mabon, pp. 150–151

## CELEBRATING MABON

This is a time to rest and catch our breath in order to make ready for the winter. Fresh fruit and berries are prepared and stored, or made into food that can be canned, bottled, pickled, relishes or wine, or, these days, put in the freezer. Homes should be checked to ensure any repairs are done before the winter weather makes anything worse, and gardens and greenhouses should be tidied and settled for the year (where practical, leave fallen leaves to return to the soil to enrich it).

Then raise a toast to the successes of this past summer!

# SAMHAIN

Cross-Quarter Day • Hallowe'en • October 31–November 1

**Samhain is the final cross-quarter day of the year, the seventh sabbat, and the start of the Dark Half of the year. The name may come from the Irish for "summer's end." Like Beltane, Samhain is a time when the veil between the world of the living and the dead grows thin and communication—and sometimes access—between the worlds is possible. This is the final harvest of the year, the Harvest of Nuts and Berries, and was at one time the first day of the New Year.**

Traditionally, bonfires were lit, and the cattle brought home from the summer pastures to their winter shelters. Samhain is the end of the growing season as the Earth enters into her temporary sleep of death, resting before the cycle of nature begins again with the emergence of the spring growth.

## THE SAMHAIN ALTAR

The colors of Samhain are black, orange, and purple. Altars are decorated with these colors, with apples, nuts—hazel, acorn, conkers—and berries, with black and orange candles, and a chalice filled with red grape juice. Also placed on the altar are photographs of the deceased if we have them. To honor deceased pets, put out a bowl of animal-appropriate food—foxes, hedgehogs, crows, and birds will enjoy the treat.

**SEE ALSO:**

Samhain Activities, pp. 118–119

Month Eleven: Samhain, pp. 154–155

## CELEBRATING SAMHAIN

This is a time to honor the ancestors, those who have gone before us—family, friends, our pets, people we love, those we respect. We light candles in remembrance and sit quietly together in contemplation of all they have given us. It's a time to reflect on all we accomplished and to dream of new beginnings. Although a solemn festival, Samhain holds within it the seeds of rebirth with the coming spring. There is always hope.

It's traditional to cook seasonal vegetables at your feast—remember to include apples in some form. It's customary in some traditions to set a place for the ancestors at your table, and cook one of their favorite meals. Conversation over the meal could mention things they liked, so as to make their spirits feel welcome.

# YULE

Quarter Day • Midwinter Solstice • December 20–23

**The Midwinter fire festival of Yule has been celebrated for millennia, and with good reason—it marks the longest night of the year, and from now on the nights grow shorter, bringing with them the hope of the spring.**

In many more recent traditions the Yuletide festival lasts from the Solstice itself until January 1, the start of the modern New Year. After the arrival of Christianity and the assumption of December 25 as Christmas, many of the original traditions—the Yule log, the Yule tree, Yuletide songs, the exchanging of presents, extravagant feasts, carousing and generally enjoying oneself—were adopted by the new religion.

There is a charming tradition that, in ancient times, the bonfires, feasting, singing, and festivities were intended to pique the sun's curiosity, so he would return after the longest night to see what all the merriment was about, and thus start the yearly cycle again.

## THE YULE ALTAR

The colors of Yule are bright red and bright green, with gold and white accents, and altars should be decorated accordingly. Candles should be red and green, and holly and mistletoe are traditional plants. Holly symbolizes immortality and the wisdom of the Holly King. Its leaves stay green and fresh when other leaves are dead or dreary. Mistletoe is symbolic of romance, fertility, and rebirth, hence the tradition of kissing beneath it. Other decorative items include a chalice of red wine—perhaps mulled with warming spices—or sherry.

**SEE ALSO:**

Yule Activities, pp. 120–121

Month Twelve: Yule, pp. 156–157

Turkey is a recent incorporation into the Yuletide celebrations. The original Yuletide meal in Europe was a roast boar, but as the large birds feed a small multitude, and are very tasty, they can be considered a perfectly suitable alternative!

## CELEBRATING YULE

Yule is a celebration of life and love in the cold, dreary depths of the winter. It closes a chapter of our lives in preparation for the opening of the next. The spirit of kindness and compassion should rule the Earth, and everyone should be treated with respect and consideration. It's also time to give to charity, both our time and physical goods, so those without a home, friends, or enough to eat can have a little relief.

Above all, it marks the promise of light and joy coming back to the world with the sun's return.

# THE GREEN WITCH

Consider which Path of witchcraft you might wish to take.
The Path of the green witch will immerse yourself in the natural world.

**Also called garden or forest witches, in the past, green witches were usually women living alone, often at some considerable distance from other people. They worked with herbs and plants they grew themselves and were often known as the wise women of the village or neighborhood, consulted for their knowledge of herbal medicine.**

Today the Path of the green witch is both popular and deeply satisfying. Green witches are in love with, and sympathetic to, the natural world in all its aspects, and have an especial affinity with all growing things. Primarily solitary witches, they are frequently skilled herbalists, gardeners, and foragers, and at their best are capable of living simply on everything the wild world provides.

They will walk or cycle rather than drive, love being barefoot out of doors, feeling the connection of human skin to the ground beneath (albeit preferably sandy, grassy, or smooth rather than gritty, prickly, or thorny) and always prefer to be outside rather than in an enclosed indoor space. They are deeply in tune with the turn of the seasons, and can sense the ever-changing energy of the world.

**SEE ALSO:**

The Growth of a Kitchen Witch, pp. 122–123

Month Seven: Take a Breath, pp. 146–147

A green witch often has their own garden, some or all of which is dedicated to growing the plants needed for their own purposes. This may be for food, but is often for making oils for herbal medicine or aromatherapy. They will also have a good idea of places in the area where they may find the plants they can't grow—not all plants will grow in all soils, and not everyone has the room for a willow or hazel tree in their garden!

The green witch will make the time to experiment with their plants, learning how to work a little nature magic. They will embrace the energies of the Earth, and respect all living things, understanding that everything works together in the marvel of creation. They may make their own tools out of natural materials found on walks or when preparing the garden beds. In a quiet way, the original green witch was also the original environmentalist. Today's green witches follow in that quiet but essential Path, loving Mother Nature with all their heart.

# THE KITCHEN WITCH

Consider taking the Path of the kitchen witch, immersing yourself in activities related to hearth and home.

Also known as a hearth or cottage witch, a kitchen witch concentrates their Craft on making the home, and especially their kitchen and everything that takes place there, a safe, secure, and sacred space for all who enter. The kitchen witch will focus particularly on the preparation, cooking, and serving of food as a ritual, as an act of the greatest love. Their greatest aim is to nourish the world, ceremonially in the persons of their loved ones and those they cook for, but they may often volunteer to help out feeding the homeless and hungry, too.

They will have their own tools, which no one else is allowed to touch, dedicated solely to the art of creating wholesome, healthy sustenance, and will often keep an eye out for the unusual or eccentric implement to assist them. The cook with a small, very sharp sickle for harvesting herbs is more than likely to be a kitchen witch—even if they don't refer to themselves as such.

There may well be a crossover between green witch and kitchen witch, as the kitchen witch will very often have a small plot in the garden for vegetables and fruit—sometimes the more unusual varieties—or at least a few pots of herbs, that they will use to work their culinary magic.

**SEE ALSO:**

The Craft of a Kitchen Witch, pp. 124–125

Month Ten: Time to Reflect, pp. 152–153

A meal cooked by a kitchen witch will feel like a feast, served with overflowing love. It will be healthy, with all homemade ingredients, homegrown if possible, and deeply satisfying. The kitchen itself will be scrupulously clean and feel a little like a shrine. All in all, an invitation for a meal from a kitchen witch is to be honored and deeply enjoyed.

## THE HEDGE WITCH

Hedges are boundaries between areas or spaces, and a hedge witch in this context is a witch who is able to "jump hedges," literally crossing between the normal world and the spiritual world. They are also able to send messages between the worlds.

It is said that they are proficient in astral travel—a consciously directed out-of-body experience when the Self (soul, spirit, etheric body) leaves the physical body and travels to a different dimension, to commune with other souls or pass messages to those who have died. It may be that the traditional image of a witch flying on a broomstick was a misunderstanding of this concept.

Such a hedge witch tends to focus on spiritual work rather than the physical here and now. They practice lucid dreaming, astral projection, and spiritual healing. They share some similarities to shamans, although this is usually more concerned with directing Otherworld energies to this world for healing. While this aspect of the Craft is beyond the scope of this book, there are plenty of outside resources if you are interested in finding out more.

# ECLECTIC WITCHCRAFT

An overview of some of the more recent and unusual forms of the Craft of the Wise.

Much of what we've dealt with so far has been traditional witchcraft. While still vitally relevant today, it does not always take into account the everchanging nature of the modern world. On the following pages, we'll consider alternative forms of the Craft of the Wise that have developed in recent years.

## COSMIC WITCHCRAFT

Originally an offshoot of astrology, today this variety of the Craft is also involved with the physical reality of advances in space exploration. Now that humans have landed on and explored part of the moon, sent exploratory probes to land on Mars, launched long-term probes to the outer solar system and beyond, our knowledge and experience of life has expanded further the dreams of those who came before. Cosmic witchcraft uses the new knowledge in rituals, calling on cosmic energies to work its magic.

**See also:**

Choosing a Path, pp. 126–129

## LUNAR WITCHCRAFT

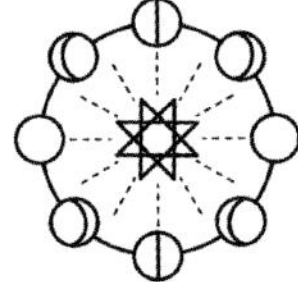

Distantly related to cosmic witchcraft is lunar witchcraft. Practitioners follow the cycles of the moon, celebrate the lunar phases, and perform rituals and moon magic at the full and dark moons. The most dedicated may conform to a lunar day of twenty-four hours and fifty minutes, starting the "day" at moonrise and ending it at moonset. Adhering to this is only possible if you don't have a normal working life, as it throws you out of sync with the normal earth day of twenty-four hours and takes an Earth month to catch up again.

## MUSIC WITCHCRAFT

Music witchcraft uses the making of music to work its magic. Of course, not all of us are musically talented, so this is used by a fairly select number of the Wise. The other side of music witchcraft is more accessible to everyone—using music to focus the mind and emotions to work whatever type of magic is required. The genre of music is up to the individual, but it should fit the overall purpose of the ritual being performed. For example, soft, romantic music for a love meditation or spell; rousing music for a Beltane ritual; the sound of rain or wind for a nature celebration. Those people who cannot do anything of worth without music playing fall into this category, even if they don't consider themselves of the Wise, and we are very fortunate these days to have thousands of years' worth of music of all kinds to choose from.

## CYBER OR TECHNO WITCHCRAFT

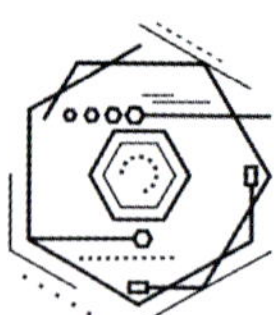

This is a very modern form of witchcraft. Have you ever met someone who somehow manages to make modern technology "behave itself"? Who only has to frown at a glitching computer or car to make it work properly again? Who understands intuitively how things work and can make them work better by touching them? You've met a technomancer. They may not call themselves such, of course, and may simply shrug, smile, and reply "Dunno!" when you ask them how they do it.

The other side of cyber witchcraft, or technomancy if you prefer, is the practitioner of the Craft who uses modern technology, mainly the Internet, to consciously work their magic. Much of this is in the form of instructional websites explaining Craft practices, rituals, and how to create and cast spells. It's not general practice (yet) to send spells or incantations across the Internet, but it may become so in time to come.

The technomancer's altar is usually their computer, laptop, or tablet at the present time, although we can expect the technology to advance. A few years from now we may have HUDs (heads-up displays) we can use as altars. The Craft of the Wise should advance with the times, while holding to the basic tenets of the Craft, so as not to become redundant.

The dark side of technomancy concerns the vileness of the dark web, hackers who endanger entire populations, and the spammers and phishers who cause such misery to ordinary people. We can only hope that the threefold law catches up to them with all due speed.

**SEE ALSO:**

Choosing a Path, pp. 126–129

## SIGIL WITCHCRAFT

Primarily involved with evoking of states of mind and moods through the use of words, the greatest poets and authors of the world are—mostly without realizing it—using sigil magic. It can be woven into written text, spoken aloud, or dispersed to the world through the Internet. It's the magic that rouses crowds to determined action and celebration—or, if misused, to riots and destruction. It's hugely powerful, and must be used with care.

## ECLECTIC AND CHAOS WITCHCRAFT

To some extent these two forms are very similar. Eclectic witchcraft is essentially a "pick and choose whatever you like" practice, using elements from any and all types of magic without following any specific traditions or Path, or even honoring any deity. It's a completely individual, unique Path for anyone choosing it, and the rituals and ceremonies are equally original, devised by the practitioner. It's highly appropriate for today's Wise, when the ability to change course at a moment's notice may be required, and to some extent having the freedom to worship (or not) and practice however we choose is very liberating. It's also easier to commit whole-heartedly to your own Path if it's not being dictated by others or bound by what some may see as outdated traditions.

Chaos witchcraft is similar to eclectic witchcraft, but takes individuality even farther, making everything up as the practitioner goes along. It may be effective, but can have unforeseen repercussions (guidance is usually there for a purpose, after all).

**The choice of which Path to follow is wide and fascinating, and can lead to enlightening revelations and discoveries. Blessed be, all, and enjoy!**

PART 2

# PRACTICING WITCHCRAFT

# GETTING STARTED

**Familiarize yourself with the three key elements of witchcraft: the Wiccan rede, the threefold law, and spellwork.**

## CANDLE VISUALIZATION

Fire plays a large role in celebrating the Path, and using a candle to focus when visualizing, meditating, performing rituals, and dedicating talismans or tools is a useful habit. A white candle is the most usual, as it can be used for all purposes. It represents a blank slate, on which you can impress your own meaning. Use scented candles if you like—they can help you focus your mind on your aims.

Sit comfortably, breathe calmly, and repeat the Wiccan rede (see opposite), or your own version of it. Make it into a spell if you like—for example:

**"I will do nothing to harm any other.**
**All of my actions will work for the good.**
**Let me be wise in the ways of the Wise,**
**So might it be so, so let it be so."**

Creating a rhythm for the incantation makes it easier to remember and adds a touch of musical magic!

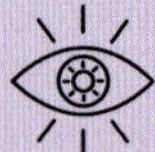

**SEE ALSO:**

Witchcraft Basics, pp. 20–23

Month One: Preparation, pp. 134–135

## CHOOSE A TALISMAN

It's not essential to use talismans in your rituals, or your life, but they can be both comforting and a useful reminder of the Path you are following. The choice is an intensely personal thing. A crystal, a piece of jewelry you never take off, an old key for symbolically unlocking the secrets of the Craft, a pen, a book, a doll, a toy animal, a figurine, a picture—anything can be used, as long as it is not too large, as you'll be carrying it with you on occasion, and handling it frequently.

Place your talisman on your altar, light a candle, speak a blessing or a spell—the one given opposite is perfectly appropriate—while focusing on your talisman. Say it three times; imagine the meaning entering the talisman as a gentle light, filling it. Gaze at it for a while, then bow your head in thanks and snuff out the candle.

Whenever you look at, or touch, the talisman, let it remind you to stay true to the Wiccan rede to "harm none."

✦ TASKS

## LEARN THE WICCAN REDE

As with all things, the more you do something, the easier it is to make it a habit. Get into the habit of repeating the Wiccan rede to yourself at least once a day—more often if you can.

**"An' it harm none, do what thou will."**

Say it before you get out of bed, and again before you settle down to sleep. Say it to yourself at lunchtime, and at dinner time. After a while it will be engrained and automatic, informing everything you choose to do, and become words to live by.

## THE THREEFOLD LAW

Light a candle, focus on the light for a few minutes. Close your eyes and consider the consequences of failing to adhere to the threefold law. Think about the implications given on p. 22, of stealing or letting off fireworks. The most obvious thought with regard to stealing is to have someone steal from you, or from someone very important to you. Remember: our actions don't just affect ourselves. In the Craft, everything is connected. As for letting off fireworks, frightening pets or nervous people, consider how you'd feel if your pet, or the pet of someone close to you, were injured or killed by the thoughtless actions of someone else.

Now focus on the consequences of doing something truly good—visiting an elderly neighbor in hospital, baking a cake for a hard-working teacher, adopting a pet puppy, sending flowers to your mom for no reason whatsoever. Consciously make the decision to be on the side of decency and honor, for its own sake as well as to preserve yourself from harm.

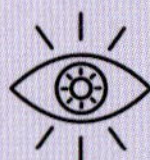

**SEE ALSO:**

Witchcraft Basics, pp. 22–23

Month One: Preparation, pp. 134–135

## SPELLWORK

Creating your own spells can make for some very enjoyable experiences. Spellwork can also go some way to defining your personal ideas and ideals about the Craft and your chosen Path.

A spell can be as simple as an affirmation:

**"I shall do right."**

But a spell can also be as complex as an intricately wrought poem. It's well worth taking some time to craft your spells carefully, being as precise as you can—although, of course, most languages aren't as precise as we might like them to be. If you like, make your spells rhyme. If you're musical, set them to music! The more thought and care you put into your spells, the more effective they'll be. They will give you the determination to work toward your goals, if nothing else. There is no reason why a spell can't also be a personal mantra.

 TASKS

## PROMOTE GOOD

Use this spell to promote good in the world around you.

**"Let me reject the bad,**
**the wrong,**
**Let me find the good, the kind,**
**In all of those around me.**
**Let my heart keep time**
**with good,**
**Let me see through evil**
**masked as logic,**
**I choose wisdom, truth**
**and insight**
**On the Path I follow."**

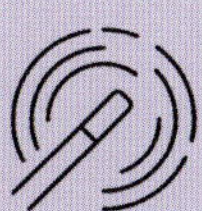

## CODE IT!

Your spells don't have to be readable to anyone but yourself. If you are mathematically inclined, you could write formulae and code to express your meaning. If you enjoy playing with words, why not come up with a language of your own. Or simply create a basic code that only you can decipher.

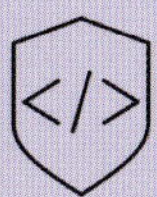

# EMBRACING NATURE

As Earth's protectors, defenders, and guardians, we need to find ways to respect Nature and celebrate the harmonious balance of her cycles.

## SALUTATION AND DEDICATION

To start with, confirm that it is your intention to do Nature no harm, by performing the following salutation and dedication.

"Hail, Mother Earth.
Bless me, your child, your defender.
I pledge myself to your service.
Where I see harm, I shall bring healing.
Where I see waste, I shall bring repair.
Where I see pain, let me bring relief.
Inspire me, Mother, show me how to live without harm,
without waste, without pain.
As you have given your gifts, freely, joyfully, without expectation,
I shall work to honor you.
Thank you for your bounty.
So might it be, so let it be, so shall it be.

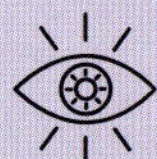

**SEE ALSO:**

The Role of Nature, pp. 24–27

Month Four: Time for Action, pp. 140–141

## CYCLES OF NATURE MEDITATION

As a baby relies on its mother for protection and sustenance, we humans rely on our Mother Earth to nourish and guard us. She provides natural foods and maintains the magnetosphere above us that keeps deadly solar radiation from devastating our planet. As we grow and develop, we can choose to be parasites, and live off her kindness without giving anything back. Or, fundamentally adhering to the threefold law, we can chose to help, to make her life better and easier.

Find ways to celebrate Nature as one season passes to the next. One option is to focus on the sabbats in order to ensure that you are living in rhythm with the natural world in accordance with the Craft of the Wise.

**ONE**
Place eight candles on your altar, one for each sabbat (see Tasks).

**TWO**
Light them and sit before them. Breathe slowly and deeply for a few minutes.

**THREE**
Repeat eight times: "I dedicate myself to following my Path. I shall do no harm. I shall honor the Mother."

**FOUR**
Feel determination welling up within you, a steady, invigorating, irresistible force for good. Let it fill and enliven you, settle within you so that you can carry it with you into the future.

**FIVE**
Come back to the outer world, bow to the altar, blow out the candles, and update your Book of Shadows. Set forth into the future with the determination to make it better for everyone.

TASKS

## BUY YOUR CANDLES

For many of the activities and tasks in this book, you will find it helps to light an appropriately colored candle. Use the list below to decide on which color is best for rituals relating to, or celebrating, the eight sabbats:

**Imbolc:** White

**Eostre:** Pink

**Beltane:** Red

**Litha:** Blue

**Lughnasadh:** Gold

**Mabon:** Orange

**Samhain:** Purple

**Yule:** Green

## A GREEN LIFESTYLE

Find ways to honor and protect nature through your actions and by making changes to your lifestyle.

- Always dispose of litter properly and responsibly. Pick up other people's litter too, when you see it.
- Recycle everything you can.
- Use natural forces in your daily life: Wash laundry on warm, sunny, or windy days and hang it outside to dry. Collect rainwater to use in your garden for pot plants.
- Stop using a hairdryer.
- Grow some of your own food, without using any chemicals.
- Feed the birds. Leave food out for wildlife if it's safe to do so. Cat or dog food are the best options for wild creatures.
- Buy the highest eco-rated, energy-saving electrical items you can afford. When not using them, switch them off.
- Support local businesses and growers, especially those using organic methods. Buy fairly traded food and materials where you can.
- Walk when you can, cycle if it's safe, use public transport wherever possible—especially "green" transport, such as bio-fueled buses. Consider electric or hybrid cars if buying, or at least try to buy the least polluting vehicle you can afford.
- Be aware of your responsibility to other people. When it comes to everyone's health, listen to the experts, not the conspiracy theorists, and take remedial action to protect everyone, not just yourself.

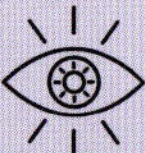

**SEE ALSO:**

The Role of Nature, pp. 24–27

Month Four: Time for Action, pp. 140–141

## NATURAL DISTRACTIONS

There is no escaping the technology of the digital age we are living in—cell phones and the Internet aren't going to go away any time soon. Still, whenever you can, close down, turn off your phone, and get outside. Look at natural things. Enjoy the sounds of birdsong or bees. Smell flowers. Interact with other human beings—you'll all feel happier for it.

## DO ONE THING

So much of the advice is basic common sense. But it is also fundamental to following the Path, especially if yours is that of the green witch (see pp. 70–71). But it's easy to slip back into old, wasteful, thoughtless ways. To start with, pledge to do just one thing each day to honor Mother Earth. Then add another, and another, until you find yourself automatically following your Path. If you like, say a short phrase as you perform an activity, along the lines of: "I do this in the name of Mother Earth." With a little practice, you'll soon find new habits becoming engrained.

✦ TASKS

## JOIN A CAUSE

Join a campaign to work toward making a better world. Online "slacktivism" is easy, does no harm, and at least shows that people care. If possible, join local environmental groups for stream and river cleaning, tree planting, rubbish collection, beach cleaning. It's free exercise, and doing something positive will make you feel better. Mother Earth will love you for it, too!

# YOUR SACRED SPACE

**Everyone needs a sacred space of their own and now is the time to think about what that means to you.**

A sacred space is somewhere you feel safe and protected. It is a place where you can be yourself and free to worship as you wish, without having to worry about what anyone else thinks. Decide what "sacred" means to you. You may prefer to use your space purely for rituals or worship, or as a space for meditation and self-examination, or maybe as a space in which you can practice dance, or yoga, or your favorite exercise if you prefer active meditation.

## FIND YOUR SPACE

Your space doesn't have to be very big, but hopefully it will be somewhere in your home. If a whole room is out of the question, find an area where you will be out of the way of other people and away from distractions. A corner of your bedroom would be ideal, and the area immediately around your altar is fine. If your space happens to be in a room you share with others, arrange to have it to yourself at certain times. Simply rededicate it whenever you come to use it. A space in your garden is also fine, and it can feel very special to have a small sacred circle to use at will.

Use your space whenever you need to, to rejuvenate your spirit and soothe your mind. Joyfully celebrate the sabbats there, if meeting up with others isn't an option.

Ultimately, of course, your sacred space is within you, and as you progress along the Path, you will grow closer and closer to it, until you carry it within you everywhere we go. Therein lies a peace that no one can erase.

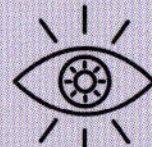

**SEE ALSO:**

Sacred Spaces, pp. 28–29

The Sacred Circle, pp. 30–31

## MAKE IT PERSONAL

Decorate your space with things you find calming, beautiful, and inspirational. Shells, candles, crystals, statuettes, figurines, inspiring quotes or poems, fragrancers—the choice is boundless. Keep adding things whenever you find something else that moves you. Put objects on your altar and keep them close so that you can touch, handle, or read them frequently.

## DEDICATE YOUR SPACE

Your dedication can be as simple or as elaborate as you like. It can even change according to need or whim every time you use it:

**"I dedicate this space to myself.**
**May it bring me peace, understanding, self-realization, self-compassion.**
**I dedicate this space to making my dreams come true, to learning about myself and my Path.**
**I dedicate this sacred space to wisdom, truth, and love.**
**So shall it be."**

 TASKS

## MAKE A SACRED CIRCLE

Even though an outdoor space is likely to be difficult to use at certain times of the year, it can feel very special to have a small sacred circle to visit at will. Gather sticks or twigs to create a temporary circle for each of the fall and winter sabbats. Or find a collection of stones for creating something that will endure through all four seasons of the year.

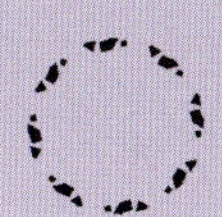

# CHOOSING YOUR TOOLS

Gather together your tools for practicing the Craft and, if you can, make them yourself, learning about their uses and meanings as you do so.

## YOUR BOOK OF SHADOWS

It's important to decide what sort of book is right for you. It will be a constant companion on your Path so it needs to feel right. Should it be a traditional book with blank pages and leather covers? A fancy exercise book? A lockable diary? Or one you've made yourself?

Once you have decided, and the book is in front of you, write a dedication on the first page, saying the words aloud as you write them.

Here are some suggestions for your dedication ritual:

**"I dedicate this book to my search for knowledge and wisdom. I entrust my thoughts and feelings to its pages. May it be blessed with the truth."**

**"Be my companion on my Path. Show me the truth of myself. Teach me what I need to know for fulfillment."**

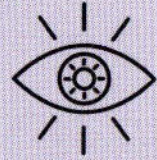

**See also:**

Tools of the Craft, pp. 32–33

Elemental Tools, pp. 34–35

## THE PERFECT ALTAR

Think about the sort of altar you want to use for practicing your craft. Is there a room in your house where you can dedicate a small corner, perhaps with a little table that you can keep specifically for your tools and your Book of Shadows?

Or perhaps outdoors is best for you. If you have a garden, is there a little nook you can use for yourself? Think about constructing a small altar using a tree stump, some wood or rocks, or use a little outdoor table. Be sure to keep your book and tools dry indoors.

Once you have chosen the right spot, make a dedication to your altar, along the following lines:

**"Support my endeavors, I pray you, and lend me your steadiness to keep me on my Path."**

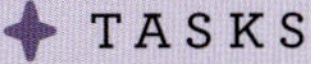

TASKS

### WRITE A BOOK ENTRY

Once a week, preferably on the same day and at the same time, set aside a little personal time to update your Book of Shadows with your recent experiences. Be sure, also, to update your book with every sabbat you celebrate. When you make an entry in the book, finish the ritual by repeating a short affirmation—for example, "This is my chosen Path."

### DECORATE YOUR ALTAR

Regularly decorate your altar with grasses, flowers, or leaves, depending on what is natural to the season, and with candles on the sabbats. This is a wonderful way of attuning yourself to the cycle of the year.

## YOUR WAND

Look for a small wooden branch or a thick stick on a walk. It doesn't need to be perfectly straight—our mental processes rarely are, after all—but it needs to feel comfortable in your hand. You can always smooth off any rough or prickly patches.

Alternatively, perhaps you will find a long, thin quartz wand that feels just right. To make it more comfortable to hold you can wrap fabric—a piece of leather or felt—around the blunt end.

You could try designing your own wand, using a length of copper pipe with a crystal in one end and a copper cap in the other.

Dedication ritual:

**"May my mind be as sure and resolute as this wand. I dedicate it to enlarging my mind and understanding."**

## YOUR ATHAME

A paperknife is probably the safest choice, although if you have chosen the Path of a green witch or a kitchen witch, a garden or kitchen knife will have special resonance.

Either way, perhaps chose a knife with a decorative handle or one made from a natural material—wood, stone, crystal.

Dedication ritual:

**"May my will be as strong and as keen as this knife. I dedicate it to making my desires clear and my dreams come true."**

## YOUR CHALICE

From a simple hand-thrown pottery cup to an elaborate carved and encrusted goblet, the choice of chalice is entirely up to you as long as it's safe to drink from. It should be something you find meaningful and beautiful. Fill with water for the dedication, and drink the water when done.

Dedication ritual:

**"May my emotions be as calm and as still as this water. I dedicate this cup to revealing to me the truth about myself and those around me."**

## YOUR PENTACLE

You may find a suitable pebble or rock on a walk through a wood or on a beach, or maybe you have a favourite crystal. As long as it appeals to you and reminds you of the earth, it is perfectly suitable. It can be as large or small as you are comfortable with.

Dedication ritual:

**"May my life be as strong and as stable as this stone. May it remind me to do what is right, always."**

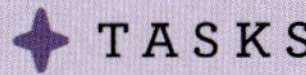

TASKS

## PERSONALIZE YOUR TOOLS

- Your basic wand can be decorated to your own taste with thin wire, fabrics, small crystals, feathers . . . pretty much anything you like as long as it's safe to handle. Consider incorporating the symbol for the air element.
- Making a small felt or leather sheath to cover your athame blade when not in use and decorate it with the symbol for the fire element.
- If your chalice is made of wood, metal, or glass, consider having it engraved with motifs of your own design, or with the symbol for the water element.
- Inscribe, paint, or draw the earth element on your pentacle.

# CALLING ON THE ELEMENTS

**The natural elements can help you focus on different aspects of your life; use these rituals and spells as inspiration for creating your own.**

## SPIRIT MEDITATION

You are spirit, the center of your circle, your sacred space. Decorate your altar with the appropriate tools for your purpose, the goal you wish to achieve. Make sure you're physically comfortable and have no distractions. Light a white or silver candle on your altar. Sit and breathe deeply for a few minutes, counting as you breathe to calm and settle your mind. Focus on aligning yourself with the elements: visualize fire for fire, clouds or wind for air, the sea for water, an image of the world, or a wood, for earth. Mentally bow to each image, giving it a mental blessing, before gently leaving the meditation.

## MEDITATION FOR SUCCESS

Air magic is recommended for cleansing and healing. Its symbol, the wand, represents the intellect. Before a test or exam, or if you are suffering from a mild ailment (hayfever, a cold), or if you're facing something that requires a lot of concentration, light a yellow candle and/or some incense on your altar. Sit for a moment, focusing on the task ahead, and gradually build up your determination to succeed in your task. Try this spell:

**"Hail, element of air, bringer of the wind that cleanses,
Bless me, I entreat you, with your clarity.
Brighten my mind, freshen my understanding,
And grant me success.
So might it be."**

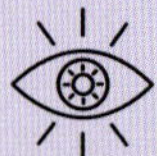

**SEE ALSO:**

Elemental Tools, pp. 34–35

Elemental Magic, pp. 38–41

## SUMMONING WILLPOWER

A little fire magic may help you if you have to make some tough decisions. Light a red candle and pace slowly back and forth or around your altar if space allows, letting your willpower and determination build with each slow, deliberate step. Visualize yourself becoming stronger-willed and more determined. Try this spell:

**"Hail, bright flame, symbol of my power to succeed.
Bless me with your strength
So let it be."**

## TRANQUILITY MEDITATION

For soothing a nervous disposition, easing the stress of a difficult day, or the need for a peaceful sleep, with calming—or prophetic—dreams, spend a few minutes watching the reflection of the light of candles on your altar shimmering in a bowl of water. Breathe deeply, and feel yourself relaxing, your mind shimmering like the water, as cool and calm as a hidden lake. Try this spell:

**"Sweet water of life, help me sleep, and in that sleep,
Let me find peace and understanding.
So let it be."**

## EARTH'S BOUNTY

We walk upon the Earth. It's our firm foundation, the element with which we spend much time, and from which our food is grown. Decorate your altar with green and copper-brown leaves and candles, sprinkle a little salt, and bow three times in thanks to the Earth and all her bounty. Sit and meditate on the strength of the world, and how you can best draw it in and use it for good.

A spell for Earth:

**"I greet you, Earth on which I live,
I thank you for your support, and pledge mine to you.
Grant me the sense and strength to deal decently
With everyone and everything I touch,
Let me never forget where I came from.
So might it be."**

# WORKING WITH COLOR

It's time to play with colors, to explore their effects and decide how you wish to use them when practicing the Craft.

Everyone has their favorite colors, though these may change with time or depending on the situation. Always keep in mind the basic associations covered in Part 1, then try experimenting. The following exercises can be performed alone or with friends or alone. It can be interesting, enlightening, and fun to see how others react.

## COLOR EXPERIMENTS

### PASSIONATE RED

- Invite friends to a feast that celebrates all things red—red foods and drinks: red grape juice, pomegranate, beetroot, and red wine. Encourage everyone to wear red and see how people thrive on the energy of the event.
- For spells and rituals that require passion and energy, decorate your altar with red candles, flowers, fruits, and vegetables.

### WARM ORANGE

- Host an event around a bonfire on a beach at sunset. Witness the effect the mellow rays of the setting sun have on everyone present and see how people exude warmth themselves.
- When performing spells and rituals, conjure warmth by wearing orange clothes and decorate your altar with orange candles, flowers, and fruit.

### VITAL YELLOW

- Spend some time in the sun for a boost to your vitality. If you have an outdoor altar, decorate it with yellow candles and flowers, and spend a little time meditating in sunshine.
- Perform a visualization in which the goddess and the god are wrapped in sunshine, and all around them shines a gentle yellow light.

### GROUNDING GREEN

- Schedule a picnic with friends, somewhere green and grassy like a local park. Bring plenty of green foods: lettuce, cucumber, apples, green grapes, avocado, kiwi fruit, spring onions, and watercress to create a cool, earthy vibe.

### TRANQUIL BLUE

- Spend time outdoors, by water of any kind. Gaze up at the sky and imagine yourself a bird high up in the blue, soaring without a care.
- For spells and rituals that require a calm atmosphere, wear blue and place a blue candle on your altar as a focus for contemplation. Feel the serenity bubbling through your mind and spirit.

### SPIRTUAL PURPLE

- Decorate your altar completely in purple, with purple candles as the only light. Let the light shine through a glass filled with purple liquid—grape juice or wine. Use it as a focus for contemplation on how to improve your creativity on your Path.

TASKS

## KEEP A RECORD

Be sure to note all of your results and discoveries in your Book of Shadows. Through learning what color magic can accomplish, you will know how to use it wisely in future.

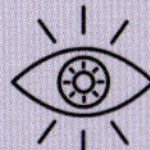

**SEE ALSO:**

The Magic of Color, pp. 42–43

# WAYS WITH HERBS

Explore the many different ways of working with herbal plants in your Craft

**When dealing with herbs and spices, always be careful in the first instance. Some people can be allergic to, or intolerant of, the most unlikely natural ingredients. Also, do not rely on herbal magic to cure serious ailments—always see a doctor or specialist.**

Try always to have basil, parsley, oregano, mint, chives, and yarrow growing in your garden or on your windowsill. These, with lavender, camomile, and marjoram (fresh or dried), provide a herb for almost all rituals and magic you might like to try at home.

## DEDICATION TO THE NATURAL WORLD

Whenever you work with plants—for ritual celebrations or in the kitchen—remember to make a short dedication to the natural world.

**"Hail, Mother Earth, Goddess of all things green and good!**
**Teach me, I entreat you, to learn with wisdom,**
**To harvest wisely,**
**And to use your bounty to make the world healthy!**
**So let it be."**

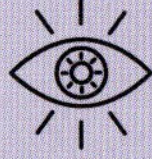

**SEE ALSO:**

The Magic of Herbs, pp. 44–45

## HERBAL TEAS

Herbal tea is the easiest starting point on your journey of discovery. Use mint, to aid digestion and ease stomach discomfort, and camomile, to aid relaxation. Try basil to inspire you, jasmine to enhance your spiritual awareness, rose to bring more love into your life, and honeysuckle flowers to attract prosperity and uplift your spirit.

## RITUAL FOR GOOD LUCK

Gather daisies, basil sprigs, lavender, heather twigs, and yarrow. Place them on your altar, light a white candle (anointed with your preferred oil), and sit for a moment, reflecting on the sort of good luck you would like to welcome into your life. Raise your hands, and speak your wish:

**"I am your child, great Mother Goddess,**
**great Father God.**
**As I love you, bestow your love upon me.**
**Grant me good luck, let all my happiest**
**dreams come true.**
**Blessed be, so let it be."**

## HERB PILLOWS

Fill palm-sized fabric sachets with dried lavender, rosemary, or rose petals. Kept beside your bed, they will aid sleep with their tranquilizing fragrance. Try this spell for a good night's sleep:

**"Hail, lavender, for healing of my body,**
**Hail, rose, for healing of my spirit,**
**Hail, rosemary, for healing of my mind.**
**Bless my sleep, and may my dreams be blameless.**
**So let it be."**

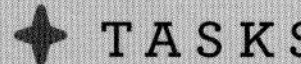

### TASKS

## BREW TEAS

To make a herbal brew, use three tablespoons of fresh herb per one cup of water. Experiment with a little more or a little less herb to adjust the flavor. If using dried herbs, use one tablespoon of herb per one cup of water. Place the herbs in a cup and pour on boiling water. Cover with a lid to keep in the volatile oils.

**Caution:** most herbs should not be taken therapeutically by children, pregnant women, or for serious health conditions without medical or herbalist consultation.

## SCENTED WATER

Collect fragrant petals, crush them, and add them to a jar of warm water. Seal the jar and shake it vigorously several times a day for a couple of weeks. Experiment until you find one you particularly like, then splash it on whenever you feel like lifting your spirits. Wear it when celebrating the sabbats.

# WAYS WITH OILS

Explore the many different ways of working with natural oils in your Craft.

## FOR YOUR ALTAR

Keep a fragrancer of some sort on your altar. Reed diffusers with your chosen fragrance oil are an excellent, easy-care option. For rituals in which candles play a part, you can also use a ceramic fragrancer with a tealight under it, which makes for a stronger perfume.

## FOR RITUALS AND SABBATS

It's a good idea to have essential oils of basil, bergamot, cedarwood, grapefruit, juniper, lavender and pine. These cover most of the basic fragrances and provide a good start for exploring mixtures of fragrance. Add more exotic oils as you become more experienced— ylang-ylang, patchouli, lemongrass, and eucalyptus, for example.

Start your work with a dedication, a silent request for inspiration from the spirits of the plants is suitable. If you're designing a ritual oil to dab onto your candles or use in a fragrancer for a sabbat, choose oils that symbolize the time of year or the nature of the festival (see Task).

As your knowledge and experience grow, you will be able to create your own, but here are a few examples to set you on your way.

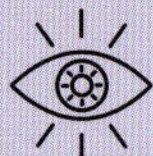

**SEE ALSO:**

The Magic of Oils, pp. 46–47

## MOON MAGIC

Juniper, jasmine, lavender, and sage are the most appropriate oils for moon magic, which will usually involve rituals to attract love, purify the body, and learning how to work more closely with the cycles of the natural world. Place lunaria seedpods on the altar for rituals. Try this spell:

**"As you wax and wane, Mother Moon, and are reborn,**
**May I also wake and sleep in tune with your peace.**
**So might it be."**

## A SPELL FOR LOSS

For easing the pain of a passing loved one, cypress, yarrow, myrrh, and oregano oils are most effective. Put a couple of drops onto your hands and sit with eyes closed, bringing to mind all that you loved most about those who have gone and recite the following:

**"Farewell, [name], may you find peace,**
**Bless me, who will miss your kindness/wisdom/ playfulness,**
**And let me be mindful of all you accomplished.**
**Let me honor your name and your life.**
**Until we meet again,**
**Blessed be."**

## FOR PROTECTION

When handling a damaging situation, oils of pine, lemongrass, rosemary, and patchouli are appropriate. Use them to anoint yellow candles, and to ask for the Sun God's assistance, place sunflowers on your altar.

**"Hail, Great God, in whose light all evil stands exposed. Grant me your power to stand firm, to resist taking the easy way, and to prevail against wrongdoing and falsehood. So let it be."**

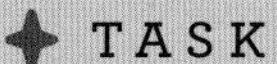

## SABBAT SCENTS

Opt for the following oils or incense on your altar when celebrating the sabbats:

**Imbolc:** Lily of the valley, pine, or citrus

**Eostre:** Toffee or chocolate, lavender or primrose

**Beltane:** Patchouli, ylang-ylang, or amber

**Litha:** Orange, rosemary, or rose

**Lughnasadh:** Ginger, cinnamon, or sandalwood

**Mabon:** Nutmeg, clove, or woodsmoke

**Samhain:** Myrrh, vetiver, frankincense

**Yule:** Jasmine, gardenia, or cedarwood

# HONOR YOUR DEITIES

**Call upon the Threefold Goddess, the Horned God, and the Green Man to contemplate wholeness, the cycle of the Earth, and the passing of time**

When honoring the goddess it is useful to consider which of her three aspects you feel most in tune with—and that aspect does not necessarily need to resemble you physically. For example, a sprightly, playful senior can feel best attuned to the Maiden, or a particularly wise, experienced youngster may feel more aligned with the Crone. And always remember, you don't have to narrow down your choice to just one, but can relate to several incarnations of the Threefold Goddess, depending on what is happening in the moment.

## GODDESS TALISMAN

There are goddess talismans available to buy from a variety of outlets, in the shape of jewelry for wearing to figurines for the altar. The simplest image is the traditional waxing-full-waning moon image, which encompasses the whole of the Threefold Goddess in one symbol. When you find one you like, place it on your altar and ask the Goddess to bless it, then wear it as often as you can.

## GODDESS DEDICATION

Memorize this dedication to use whenever you feel the need to call on the Threefold Goddess for support.

**"Blessed be, great Goddess.**
**I ask your help in becoming the best I can be,**
**To honor You in all I do,**
**And bring honor to Your name.**
**So let it be."**

**SEE ALSO:**

Deities of the Craft, pp. 48–51

## GODDESS CONTEMPLATION

**ONE**

Light three candles on your altar—one for each manifestation of the Threefold Goddess: Maiden, Mother, and Crone. They can be any color: you may feel green or pink is best for the Maiden, red or gold for the Mother, and silver or black for the Crone. White is an appropriate fallback, representing the blank slate from which your inner need can make itself known.

**TWO**

Visualize the Threefold Goddess. Imagine each of her aspects in the way that feels best to you. Energetic, playful child or stubborn, determined teen? Strong, pregnant woman or loving, nursing new mother? Powerful, forthright matriarchal elder or peaceful, understanding, compassionate wisewoman?

**THREE**

Imagine what they would say, how they would greet you. Contemplate which one, or more, you would get on with better—or worse—and consider how much you currently resemble them, or would like to resemble them. Ask them for their blessing, and welcome them into your life.

Each aspect has much to teach every one of us. Remember that as you go about your daily life. There's no harm in asking yourself how your own Goddess aspect would act in any given situation.

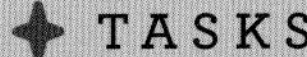

TASKS

## DO SOME RESEARCH

You may find it helpful to research the different names and associations of the Threefold Goddess before engaging in these exercises, in order to identify which manifestations you are most in tune with.

## MAKE IT PERSONAL

Make your own talisman to wear or carry around with you. Depending on your skills, you could fashion a simple waxing-full-waning moon shape from wood or clay to wear as a pendant. You could even have the motif tattooed on your body, if that's your preference, but be absolutely certain before making any such permanent changes.

## HORNED GOD COMTEMPLATION

The Horned God is a masculine figure, but just as the goddess is open to anyone of any gender, so is the god. Try to find images of his appearance—he has fewer manifestations than for the goddess, but they will help with visualization.

**ONE**
Light a large green candle on your altar.

**TWO**
Visualize the Horned God. Imagine each of his aspects in the way that feels best to you. Strong, wild hunter? Fatherly, compassionate figure? A satyr? A grim, determined businessman who puts up with no nonsense? A magnificent deer, forever racing ahead of you, calling you onward?

**THREE**
Imagine how each would greet you and what they would say. Contemplate which one you would get on with better—or worse—and consider how much you are currently like him, or would like to be like him.

**FOUR**
Ask them for their blessing, and welcome the Horned God into your life.

## HORNED GOD TALISMAN

The simplest image to symbolize the Horned God has much in common with that for the goddess and is available as jewelry of many kinds. When you find something suitable, place it on your altar and ask the Horned God to bless it, then wear it often.

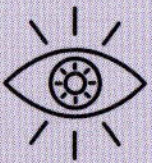

**SEE ALSO:**

Deities of the Craft, pp. 48–51

## HORNED GOD DEDICATION

Memorize this dedication to use whenever you feel the need to call on the Horned God for support.

**"Hail, great Horned God!**
**Come to me, bless the wildness and willingness and strength within me!**
**Let me be bold and brave**
**To defend the Earth and all I love.**
**So let it be."**

## GREEN MAN TALISMAN

The Green Man can be seen as a less aggressive, less overpowering figure than the Horned God—a gentler symbol of spring rebirth and the cycle of the year. There are numerous items of jewelry of the Green Man—mostly varieties of pendants in the form of foliate heads, and many of them very attractive.

To meditate on the Green Man, gaze at your Green Man symbol, imagine the leaves and vines surrounding him stirring gently in the breeze. He is a kindly spirit, a mellow God, who spreads his bounty across the world in spring, allowing us to live for another year. Visualize him blessing you.

Carry your talisman at all times to remind you of the importance of caring for the natural world.

## GEEN MAN DEDICATION

**"Hail, gentle God, bringer of the grain and grass and flowers of the spring.**
**Let me do no harm to our beautiful world.**
**Let me protect her and love her, to honor you.**
**So let it be."**

### ✦ TASKS

## CELEBRATE BELTANE

To celebrate the sabbat of Beltane, create a foliate head—carved, molded, or fashioned from wood and branches found on a walk. Hang it on a garden fence or place it on your altar, as a symbol of nature and its rebirth every year.

# IMBOLC ACTIVITIES

**A celebration for spring, Imbolc is the time for new beginnings, and that includes spring cleaning.**

## WELCOME IN THE SPRING

Before celebrating this fire festival, take the time to clean your home. Symbolically sweep winter out of the door, and welcome in the spring. Clear out your wardrobe and give anything you don't want to charity. Clear through the refrigerator, freezer, and store cupboard, get rid of anything out of date or past its "use by," and prepare a meal with anything that's close to being out of date. Add ginger to help reignite the fire within. Use your imagination to create something unusual and new!

## SEASONAL CONTEMPLATION

Imbolc is a time to clear your mind as well as your house. There are several symbols you can use for contemplation and meditation.

- Swans mate for life, and represent faithful love and loyalty. Place a picture or a figure of two swans on your altar to attract fidelity and love into your life this year. Focus on their beauty, their grace, and the ferocity and strength with which they defend their mate and family.
- The snowdrop is one of the first flowers to appear in the spring after the grimness of winter, and as Brigid's flower is symbolic of new life and growth. Keep some on your altar, use them as a focus for meditation on the hope of the coming year.
- Make sure you light a white candle on your altar or in your sacred space to celebrate the festival of Imbolc. Choose a candle scented with a light, floral fragrance.

**SEE ALSO:**

Imbolc, pp. 54–55

Month Two: Imbolc, pp. 136–137

## IMBOLC TALISMANS

Swan feathers make an ideal talisman, if you can find them. Keep one on your altar or carry it with you. If you have several and are feeling particularly crafty, make them into jewelry—maybe earrings—that you can wear for festivals as a reminder of the joy of Imbolc.

The serpent is another Imbolc creature, traditionally emblematic of the Maiden aspects of the Goddess, including Brigid. It symbolizes regeneration and rebirth, and is easily obtainable in the form of jewelry. It's easy to wear and its symbolism can make it a comforting talisman to have with you at all times.

✦ TASKS

## THE BRIGID CROSS

Decorate your altar with a Brigid Cross, a charm to keep evil, fire, and hunger from your home. Traditionally made from rushes or straw (and luckiest if you can gather the materials yourself), there are online tutorials to teach you how to make your own, if you so desire. If not, a simple picture will be more than sufficient.

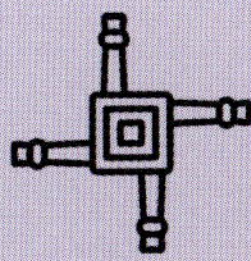

# EOSTRE ACTIVITIES

Celebrating the natural world at the peak of the spring season.

## WAYS TO CELEBRATE

- As long as the weather is favorable, this is an excellent time to get out into the natural world. Maybe plant some seeds, or take the opportunity to walk, ride, sail, or simply sit and enjoy the wonders around you.
- Eggs, honey, fresh fruit, chocolate—chocolate eggs, if you like them—and buns all have associations with the Eostre celebration. A staple of this time of year, the hot cross bun doesn't just represent the Christian cross; it also symbolizes the quartering of the year into the quarter days and the seasons, the four directions, and the elements of air, fire, earth, and water.

## SEASONAL CONTEMPLATION

This is the time to take notice of the wildlife around you. Hares aren't that common these days, but you might still catch a glimpse if you're in the right place. Wild birds are usually nesting, but you will still see them flying about searching for food. And there are a lot of bugs and caterpillars around at this time of year. If you're near water, watch ducks or seabirds. Listen to the sounds of nature; let them wash over you. Give silent thanks for the blessings of the season, for the love of friends and partners, and for the love of the goddess who grants these gifts freely. Resolve never to take her for granted.

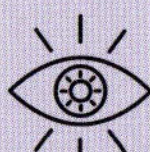

**SEE ALSO:**

Eostre,
pp. 56–57

Month Three: Eostre,
pp. 138–139

## EOSTRE TALISMAN

As with many sabbats, jewelry may be the easiest talisman to make or find. Eostre's symbols are eggs for potential, hares for happiness, butterflies for beauty, and spring flowers for the promise of the future. That gives you plenty of choices for lucky charms, earrings, necklaces, pendants, figurines, even keyrings. Dedicate your chosen talisman as a reminder to rejoice in the blessings of the spring.

## A SPELL FOR THE SPRING EQUINOX

As part of your Eostre celebrations, spend some time in your sacred space and recount this spell before meditating for a while in front of a lit candle.

**"May I be light as sunfilled air, as strong as the circle of the year,**

**Filled with joy, thankful and true, free of care on this merry day!**

**As light of spirit as a bird on the wing, may I set forth into the future,**

**Ready to take delight in its mysteries.**

**Let my mind be fruitful, my heart renewed.**

**May I grow in vigor, may my dreams be realized.**

**So let it be!"**

### TASKS

## PAINT EGGS!

Paint some eggs to decorate your Eostre altar. Green, yellow, pink, and white are the most appropriate colors, with a tiny touch of purple. Unless you have a very light touch, it's probably best to hard-boil the eggs first. If you have children, you can tell them all about Eostre while you paint the eggs.

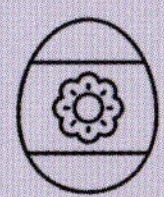

# BELTANE ACTIVITIES

Find ways to celebrate this third festival of the year, which marks the start of the growing season.

## SUN SALUTATION

As long as the weather is favorable, stand barefoot on the grass first thing in the morning, skyclad (naked) if you have the privacy and it's not too cold! Face the east, stretch your arms out to the side, hands open, and raise your head. Gaze at the sky and welcome the rising sun. Even if it's overcast or raining, the sun will rise regardless. Call out the following salutation:

**"Hail, Bel, brightest in the sky. I bid you welcome, and entreat your blessing to heal and help my life and the lives of those I love."**

Back inside, focus on warmth and comfort for a few minutes before making a start on daily life. Remember, this is a day for celebration, be determined not to let anyone darken it for you.

## AN ACTIVE MEDITATION

Beltane is the festival of love, virility, passion, and fertility. Tell a friend how much you appreciate them and how much they mean to you. Contact someone you haven't spoken to in a while and see how they are doing, and wish them well. If there are children in your family, tell them you love them. Let your love and understanding grow. If you have a partner, and the weather is favorable, and somewhere private, treat yourselves to the ancient Beltane ritual of making love outside in the open air, surrounded by the natural world. Feel the joy of the season thrill through you both, and give thanks to the goddess and the Green Man for the love you share.

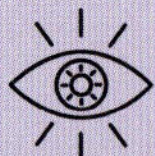

**SEE ALSO:**

Beltane, pp. 58–59

Month Five: Beltane, pp. 142–143

## A SPELL FOR BELTANE EVE

**"May I forever celebrate love and light and laughter,
Through all the years to come.
May I ever keep my love here by my side,
Thankful for their nearness and understanding.
So might it be."**

## SUN DOWN

Take a moment before bed to close your eyes and think about what the sun means to you. The source of life on Earth? A fierce protector of the planet? A friend spreading his bounty throughout time and space? Think your thanks for all he gives, and envisage his softer, evening face as you go to sleep.

✦ TASKS

## A NEW PROJECT

Beltane is also a good time to start new projects. Sit quietly at your altar—decorated in Beltane colors and with a lit red candle—to consider what you would like to accomplish. Resolve, before the sun sets, to make a start toward achieving your goals. Seal your decision and celebrate with buttered wholemeal bread and a glass of wine or grape juice.

# LITHA ACTIVITIES

Midsummer, the longest day and shortest night of the year, is the time for feasting, loving, and celebrating the joy of being alive!

## SUMMER SOLSTICE SALUTATION

Much depends on the weather, but there's generally a good chance of it being fine and sunny for at least part of the celebration of this sabbat. If you possibly can, stay up all night on Midsummer's Eve, enjoy wine or mead, and welcome the sunrise with a joyful salutation. If you can have friends with you, so much the better, but a solitary welcome to the Summer Solstice is perfectly fine, too.

**"Greetings to Bel and the Mother, bright and beloved on this blessed day!**
**We welcome you and all your gifts, thankfully accepted,**
**Into our hearts and minds and lives!**
**Merry meet and blessed be!"**

## WAYS TO CELEBRATE

- Your altar should be cheerfully decorated with summer flowers—especially elderflowers—oak leaves, and possibly acorns. Candles can be any color you prefer, and florally scented if possible.
- Having stayed up on Midsummer's Eve, break your fast with bread and honey and sparkling juice.
- If you can, rest or sleep in sunshine for a few hours during the day to recover from the wakeful night.
- Find time to sit at your altar and spend a few minutes thinking about all the good, positive things in your life.

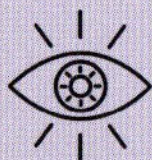

**SEE ALSO:**

Litha, pp. 60–61

Month Six: Litha, pp. 144–145

## LITHA TALISMAN

The best talisman for Litha is a sunflower, in whatever form you prefer: earrings, a bracelet charm, a pendant, a tattoo, a piece of clothing in sunflower colors—as usual, the choices are near endless. Whatever you choose, it should remind you of the sunshine and elation of this solstice. Dedicate it to the goddess and to Bel. Place your talisman on your altar, and place both hands gently over it. With your face raised to the sky, say:

**"Praise be to Bel, praise be to the Mother, praise be to the Earth that nurtures me. Bless me on this wondrous day, fill me with your joy, and bless this [name of talisman], that it may ever remind me of your gifts and your love. So might it be!"**

## IN STEP WITH NATURE

Take a gentle walk, hopefully in the sun, in the afternoon. See if you can hear bees, or recognize any birdsong. Count up the different flowers and trees you recognize.

## PERSONALIZE IT

Create your own dedications or salutations. The more personal they are to you, the more effective they will be—and the more truthfully they will honor the Goddess and the God. Be sure to record your dedications or salutations in your Book of Shadows.

# LUGHNASADH ACTIVITIES

This is the time for enjoying the summer's bounty while preparing for the coming fall and winter. There will be a lot to do in the coming months, so take pleasure in this time while you can!

## HARVEST SALUTATION

Welcome the coming harvest season with this salutation and well wishes for plentiful crops.

**"Hail, God of the Corn and Goddess of Grain!**
**Be welcome at this wondrous time,**
**And bless our work, our homes, ourselves**
**As we thank you humbly and happily for your bounty.**
**Blessed be!"**

## WAYS TO CELEBRATE

- Spend as much time out of doors as you safely can. Plant seeds and tend plants that may need deadheading or watering. Plan what to plant next.
- If you have a garden, decide what you would like it to produce next year. If you have a balcony or windowbox, or even just a few pots on a windowsill, note down whether they have been productive this year, and think about what you'd like to try next year.
- Eat hazelnuts. Try them in cakes, in chocolate, and toasted and sprinkled on salads, porridge, breakfast oats, or pasta dishes. Try hazelnut-flavored drinks—juices with fruit, syrups to add to coffee, and hazelnut liqueur. Imagine you are taking in Craft wisdom as you eat and drink!

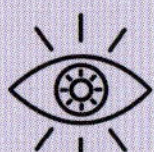

**SEE ALSO:**

Lughnasadh, pp. 62–63

Month Eight: Lughnasadh, pp. 148–149

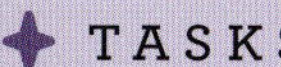

TASKS

## TREAT YOURSELF

Buy an indoor plant—preferably one that flowers. Succulents don't need a lot of care, and some produce striking blooms. African violet is easy to maintain, comes in a variety of colors, and has a long blooming season. Begonia, kalanchoe, and peace lily also flower fairly easily and don't require too much attention. Make a point of learning how to care for your plants—they will repay you with long, colorful, and productive lives, bringing cheer to the Dark Half of the year.

## SEASONAL CONTEMPLATION

Sit before an altar decorated in late summer flowers and seeds, and light a candle. Breathe calmly and deeply for a few minutes. Gaze at the flowers and seeds, and consider the cycle of their planting, growth, death, and rebirth as the year turns. Death is a certainty, but there is always a way to gain a kind of immortality in the making of something to be remembered by, in starting a family, or possibly in reincarnation if you believe in it. After all, in a universe that is, for all intents and purposes and from our perspective, nearly infinite, why should individual rebirth not be possible, somewhere?

## LUGHNASADH TALISMAN

Hazelnuts, of course—as jewelry, or the nut itself, to carry with you as a talisman of wisdom and careful consideration when making decisions in daily life.

# MABON ACTIVITIES

This is the time to celebrate the successes of the year, make ready for winter, and celebrate and mellow out with friends and family.

## FALL SALUTATION

Find ways to celebrate the fall equinox and the great feast of Thanksgiving at the end of summer. Start off with a simple salutation.

**"Hail, Child of Light! Child of the Harvest!
We thank you for your gifts of the fruits of the Earth,
May we use them wisely and well.
Blessed be!"**

## WAYS TO CELEBRATE

- Take a walk, collect berries and wild fruit—sloes, elderberries, and rosehips—and bring them back to decorate your altar.
- Eat an apple every day.
- Clear some space in your garden or windowbox, and plant some bulbs. It's traditional to plant each bulb with a wish or a hope for the year to come. Snowdrops are perfect, as they'll flower very early next spring, bringing the hope of the brightness of spring and the fertility of summer with them.
- Finish projects started earlier in the year, if possible. Maybe finish reading that book, or writing that story, or complete that drawing or painting.
- Plan what you would like to do next year—in the garden, in the house, in your life. Consider taking up a new hobby, language, sport, or course of study.

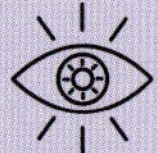

**SEE ALSO:**

Mabon, pp. 64–65

Month Nine: Mabon, pp. 150–151

## MABON TALISMAN

Apples, in whatever form are best for you. Jewelry is always a good option. If you have the space, plant an apple tree. Try to find a more unusual variety rather than the types you find in the local supermarket.

## A SPELL FOR THE FALL EQUINOX

As part of your Mabon celebrations, spend some time in your sacred space and recount this spell before meditating for a while in front of a lit candle.

**"May I be warm as fall sun, loving as the Earth,**
**Tranquil as the gentle moon, thoughtful and compassionate,**
**True to the very best of myself.**
**So let it be."**

### ✦ TASKS

## BLESSING

Create a Mabon blessing of your own and recite it as you light the candles on your altar. Keep a record of your blessing in your Book of Shadows.

## HOST A FEAST

Invite friends and family to a feast. Use as much locally grown fruit and vegetables for the meal as you can—and any that you have grown yourself over the year. Make an apple pie for the dessert, served with fresh cream.

# SAMHAIN ACTIVITIES

This festival celebrates the Harvest of Nuts and Berries; it brings an end to the summer months, and heralds a time to honor much-missed ancestors.

## SOLEMN SALUTATION

Start your celebrations with a few thoughts for those who have passed.

"Hail to those who have gone before us.
We honor you, we thank you for your gifts of life and knowledge,
And know that we will meet again in the Summerland, when the time is right.
Blessed be, merry meet, merry part, and merry meet again."

## WAYS TO CELEBRATE

- The air is usually cooler and occasionally crisper now. Get out for walks as often as you can and complete work in the garden.
- Take a little time to contemplate possible life paths ahead of you. It might be time for a change.
- Visit the graves of deceased family and friends. Leave a small offering—golden chrysanthemums are ideal—and pause for a moment, remembering their achievements and what they meant to you.

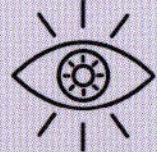

**SEE ALSO:**

Samhain, pp. 66–67

Month Eleven: Samhain, pp. 154–155

## SEASONAL CONTEMPLATION

Light a candle on your altar, and gaze at it for a few minutes, breathing evenly and calmly. Watch the movements of the flame, its subtle color changes. Think about what fire means to you. A warming presence? A source of light? A fierce weapon? Something to be afraid of? One of the primary elements, the power of the stars that give light and life to the universe? All of these and more? Consider how you can use the power of fire, spiritually, to brighten and improve your life.

## SAMHAIN TALISMAN

The most effective talisman for Samhain is very much a matter of personal choice. A locket with a picture of a loved one, the image of a raven or crow—both wise birds, carrion eaters, and in some traditions credited with connecting the world of the living with the realm of the dead—in the form of jewelry, a tattoo, or a candle.

✦ TASKS

## GRAVESIDE BLESSING

If there's a location a loved one and yourself enjoyed together, revisit it. Take a small token to leave at the site, maybe a favorite flower or a message written in ink on paper. Think for a few minutes of the happy times you spent together. Say a silent blessing before you leave.

**"Bless me, I pray, and grant me your wisdom**
**As I bless you and all you have done, all you have given the world.**
**May your rest be deep and peaceful, your wakening blessed and happy,**
**And may I see you once more, in time.**
**Blessed be, [name], with my love."**

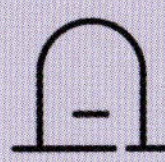

# YULE ACTIVITIES

Celebrate the longest night of the year, with this fire festival heralding the return of the Sun God

## WINTER SOLSTICE SALUTATION

The festival can last from the winter solstice until 1 January. Mark the event with this Yuletide salutation.

**"We greet you, great God of Light and Warmth, on this your rebirth day,**
**And welcome you back from your winter sleep. Bless us, bright One,**
**Fill our days with love and life, and may we always thank you**
**For your many gifts to us.**
**Merry meet!"**

## WAYS TO CELEBRATE

- It's time to meet with friends and family to celebrate the year past and anticipate the one to come. Celebrate indoors, in a warm room with candles and music, and outdoors, by a warm bonfire with mulled wine and laughter. Do both, and relish the spirit of conviviality and mellow friendship such meetings bring.
- Cook a feast (it doesn't need to be extravagant, just made with love) in honor of the god and goddess and invite friends and family. Talk about the good things that have happened in the past year, and your hopes for the coming year.
- Give to charity and make a promise to continue to do so in the coming year. A monthly donation to a charity of your choice, perhaps.

**SEE ALSO:**

Yule,
pp. 68–69

Month Twelve: Yule,
pp. 156–157

## SEASONAL CONTEMPLATION

If you can get to experience a snowy landscape, wrap up and go for a walk. If not, find images of snowflakes—pictures, photographs or jewelry—and place them on your altar. Contemplate the cold beauty of this frozen phenomenon for a few minutes. Appreciate its complexity, and the wonder of the forces that turn water into delicate jewels.

## GIFT-GIVING

Gift-giving at Yule is a much appreciated tradition. If you can make the gifts you give to others, so much the better! Have you made jam or pickle during fall? Do you knit or sew, or paint or draw? Consider making the products a gift for a friend or family member. They'll be that little bit more special. Say a blessing as you wrap them up (see p. 156), or simply wish for the recipient to have luck, love, and health in the coming year.

✦ TASKS

## A GOOD CAUSE

Take up a cause you feel deeply about. If it has promotional material, consider buying some: a WWF T-shirt, perhaps, or a 4Ocean bracelet, or just a discreet badge or button supporting Cancer Research. The choice is huge, and doing something, no matter how small, to help is both a good way to feel better about yourself and to attract good in return through the threefold law.

# GROWTH OF A GREEN WITCH

**Use the exercises on these pages to see if your Path should be that of a green witch and use them to develop activities of your own.**

## GROW A PLANT

You don't need a garden for this exercise; a windowsill will do just fine. Choose a herb—mint, thyme, basil—or an edible plant such as cherry tomatoes, green onions, radishes, all of which grow well in pots. Learn how to care for your plant. Give it a try, and enjoy the fruits (literally) of your work with plants.

## SENSE THE NATURAL WORLD

Go for a walk somewhere green. A local park is sufficient, although the farther you can get away from buildings and people the better. Fully engage your senses.

**Listen** to the wind, to birdsong, to flowing water, insects. Imagine you can hear the plants growing.

**Smell** the air and the plants around you. Pick a blade or two of grass or a leaf and sniff them. If there are flowers in the area, smell them. Sometimes flowers you might not expect have their own fragrances.

**Touch** the plants around you, feel the different textures of leaves, bark, stems, and petals.

**Taste** only those plants that you know are safe to eat. If none are available, see if you can taste the wind.

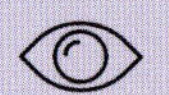

**Look** around you. Really focus on everything you can see. Appreciate the variety of colors and shapes. Feel a sense of wonder at just how gloriously complex and vivid Mother Nature can be.

**SEE ALSO:**

The Green Witch, pp. 70–71

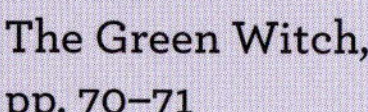

Month Seven: Take a Breath, pp. 146–147

## ENVISION MOTHER NATURE

**ONE**
Light a white candle and sit before it. Take a few deep breaths, then settle your mind on Mother Nature.

**TWO**
How do you see her? A kindly old lady surrounded by flowers? A fierce warrior woman, prepared to do anything to protect her planet? A child with eyes full of wonder? Is there a piece of music that makes you think of Mother Nature?

**THREE**
Can you draw what you see? If not, write a description or a poem about her.

✦ TASKS

## TALK TO YOUR PLANTS

Studies provide some evidence that talking to plants, especially—for some as yet undiscovered reason—if you are female, makes a plant grow faster and become more luxuriant.

## HONOR NATURE

Consider ways you can show your love for Nature. Become an environmental activist, if you aren't one already. Join public campaigns for planetary health. Support the efforts of groups trying to fight climate change and the destruction of the natural environment. She will love you for it, and you can feel at least a little happier that you've helped her.

# THE CRAFT OF A KITCHEN WITCH

Use the exercises on these pages to see if your Path should be that of a kitchen witch and use them to develop activities of your own.

## A KITCHEN SPELL

Many herbs have protective powers: dill keeps away negativity and can be used in house blessings. A bay leaf can be placed in each corner of the kitchen to protect all who enter. Garlic heals, purifies, and protects. Oregano, parsley, basil, angelica, and clover are all effective in rituals for protection. Gather your chosen herbs—any or all of the above—and place them in a bowl in the kitchen. Lay your hands on either side of the bowl, gaze at the herbs for a moment, then raise your head and say:

**"May these herbs grant their magic to my kitchen and my home,**
**May they grant that no evil may enter,**
**That all that happens here be healthful and happy,**
**That all who enter here be safe and protected,**
**And that I may use their magic to make magic of my own!**
**So let it be."**

## PERFUME MAGIC

Grow, or pick, something that can be made into a flower or herb water to splash onto your skin, or that you can macerate to make a fragrant oil. Make sure the plant is safe to use first—some plants trigger allergic reactions.

- Bruise the lavender leaves, rose petals, or elderflowers and immerse them in a bottle or jar of clean water for a few weeks with a stopper in the top.

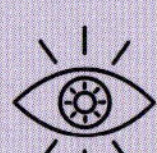

**SEE ALSO:**

The Craft of a Kitchen Witch, pp. 72–73

Month Ten: Time to Reflect, pp. 152–153

- For maceration, chop up the plant, add it to a container of warm oil (almond or sunflower), shake it regularly for several days or weeks, depending on how strong or subtle you want the perfume to be (check it regularly). Filter out the plant material and store the resulting fragrant oil in stoppered bottles. Use the oil in a room fragrancer and consider the effect. Should it be stronger? If so, leave it for longer next time, or add more plant material. Experiment with other plants. Make them with love, and when you're more proficient, perhaps give them to friends and family as gifts. Personal, handmade gifts from a kitchen witch are something very special.

## COOK A MEAL

If you've never cooked before, find a recipe for a simple soup and try it.

- Bless each tool you use: "May you work a little magic in this kitchen."
- Bless each ingredient as you prepare it: "May you be healthful and tasty!"

When it's cooked, savor it, consider how you could improve on it. A few herbs perhaps? Less salt and more pepper? Perhaps a different vegetable? Keep practicing.

If you have cooked before, try something new and a little more complicated. Invite special friends, or family members, or a partner, to eat with you. Make it a ritual, with candles and wine, perhaps. Remember to say a blessing, even if just silently, before eating.

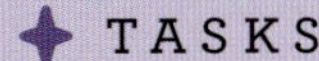

### TASKS

## GROW A PLANT FOR EATING

Decide what you want to do with your plant before starting. What meal are you going to add it to? Will it be something simple, like adding chopped basil to a spaghetti dinner, or a little more complex—mint for minted peas, maybe, or for a butter sauce. Consider green onions, lettuce leaves, tomatoes, or radishes for a salad.

# CHOOSING A PATH

Use the contemplation exercise on these pages to help you choose the right Path.

By now, you've had a chance to consider and try some of the rituals, spells, exercises, and meditations in the previous pages, and have some idea of whether the Craft of the Wise is suitable for you, your hopes and ambitions, and your way of life. Now it is time to step back for a moment, reflect on what you have learned, and decide which Path is best for you.

These days, most of the Wise draw on several different types of witchcraft. You may lean toward being a green witch, but use music to enhance your enjoyment and ability. Or perhaps you will combine green and kitchen magic to grow your own ingredients. Maybe you are an evocative and persuasive writer of poetry or speeches, but like to have hard rock playing in the background. Or perhaps you work the phases of the moon into color or elemental magic. Nothing is forbidden—an' it harm none—and the choices are plentiful.

## YOUR CHOSEN PATH

Try the following contemplation exercise to see if you can determine which Path is best for you.

- Sit calmly before your altar—at this stage your altar may be the traditional table, a stone bench, a sacred circle, an outdoor pool, or your computer—whatever suits your taste and purpose. Light white candles, fragrancers, incense, or have them flickering on your screen. Breathe deeply for a few minutes, allowing yourself to relax, and focus on the flames or smoke to calm your mind.

**See also:**

Eclectic Witchcraft, pp. 74–77

- Consider your favorite activities, books, meals, films—all the things that bring you pleasure. Think about ways to enjoy them more often, or how to incorporate them more intimately into your life. Could you write a book? Create a new, exciting meal? Devise new code for the internet? If these are too daunting right now, rein back and consider simply making more time in your life to enjoy the magic of being alive, of reading a new book, or watching a new film, of finding somewhere new to visit or discovering a new and exciting website. You can always take things slowly and steadily later.
- Contemplate the Earth, and the planet's place in the solar system. Try to imagine yourself floating above one of Earth's poles, moving outward and upward until you can make out the inner planets and the sun in the center. How far out can you go, and how does it make you feel? If it's exciting and invigorating, cosmic witchcraft might be your forte—at least in part. If it makes you feel anything else, quickly come back to Earth and say a quick thanks to her for being here to keep us all safe on the ground.

The above exercises should help bring you closer to knowing your Path. Close your eyes and breathe slowly and deeply for a few minutes, before ending the contemplation and writing it up in your Book of Shadows.

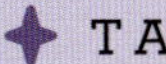 TASKS

## BOOK OF SHADOWS

Whatever Path you choose, your Book of Shadows will be an essential and irreplaceable companion. It's the one tradition that every member of the Wise should keep, no matter what their Path. Use it now to note down your experiences as you explore the Craft and decide on your Path.

## QUESTIONS TO ASK YOURSELF

If you are still uncertain which direction your Path should take, repeat some of the exercises in Part 2 again. Think about which you feel in tune with and which are not for you.

- Experiment with different musical genres. Either to listen to, or sing, or play if you're in a band or singing group. It's never too late to discover something that uplifts and invigorates you that you simply hadn't considered before.
- Consider emotional magic. Can you channel your negative emotions—anger, jealousy, fear—into positive goals? Can you use your love to create a spell for improving the lives of others?
- If you have a career, or regular work, how can you best fit your Path into your daily life? Are any of your workmates amenable to the Craft, or should you keep it a secret?
- What, ultimately, is your goal in exploring the Craft? Self-analysis and self-improvement? A way to understand, to help heal and honor the planet? An exploration into something greater than yourself? A way to explore the past and gain an understanding of the Wise? A traditional way to give direction to your life? A way to make, and keep, yourself and your loved ones healthy, safe and loved?

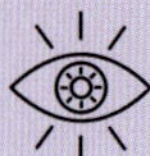

**SEE ALSO:**

Eclectic Witchcraft, pp. 74–77

Basically, unless you are a hereditary witch (and even then you can choose to make changes in your Path), you can choose whatever elements of the entirety of the Craft of the Wise appeal to you, and incorporate them into your own traditions—and if the means for what you want to accomplish don't yet exist, invent them!

**Blessed Be!**

✦ TASKS

## THE ULTIMATE TALISMAN

See if you can find a talisman (or three) that expresses what you have found out about yourself, who you are now, and what you want to achieve. Ask the cosmos to bless it, and keep it with you always.

PART 3

# YOUR WITCHCRAFT YEAR

# YOUR WITCHCRAFT YEAR

**The following pages should act as a guide for the first steps on your Path. They offer a journey, a month-by-month program for adopting witchcraft as a way of life. As the months pass, you will progress through the four seasons of the year, preparing for and celebrating the eight sabbats along the way. Building on what you have learned in Parts One and Two of the book, the activities for each month are designed to help you become more familiar with the basic concepts of the Craft and to increase your knowledge of witchcraft, of yourself, and of your environment.**

Each section offers suggestions for seasonal activities to help you focus on the cycles of the natural world and to enhance your relationship with the world around you. There are suggestions for spells and blessings that you can perform to accompany some of the exercises. Use them as inspiration to create spells, blessings, and rituals of your own. Use the write-in sections to keep a track of your progress. Hopefully, by the time you have traveled through the book, many of the suggestions contained within will have become habitual—good, wholesome activities that you return to again and again simply because they give you pleasure.

If any of the suggested activities are not for you, you are under no obligation to try them. This is your Path, and you should follow it the way your heart tells you to. Take what is written here and make it your own.

## THE WHEEL OF THE YEAR

The Craft of the Wise uses the Wheel of the Year, which runs from the Imbolc sabbat through the Yule sabbat and back to Imbolc. The month each festival falls in, in the Western calendar, will depend on which hemisphere you live in. While Yule (the midwinter solstice) in the north is in December, in the southern hemisphere, Yule falls in June; Litha (the midsummer solstice) falls in June in the north, and December in the south. Owing to their meanings and significance, it's important to celebrate the sabbats at the time they happen wherever you are in the world.

## THE NORTHERN HEMISPHERE

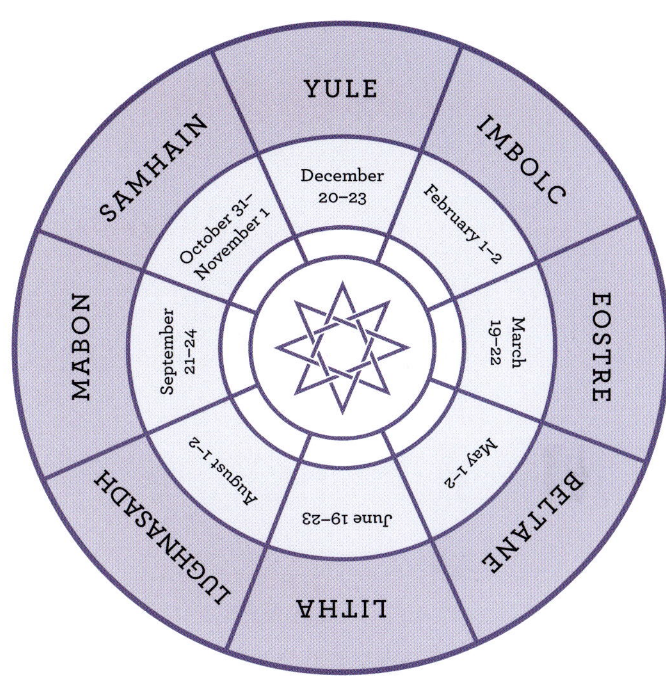


## THE SOUTHERN HEMISPHERE

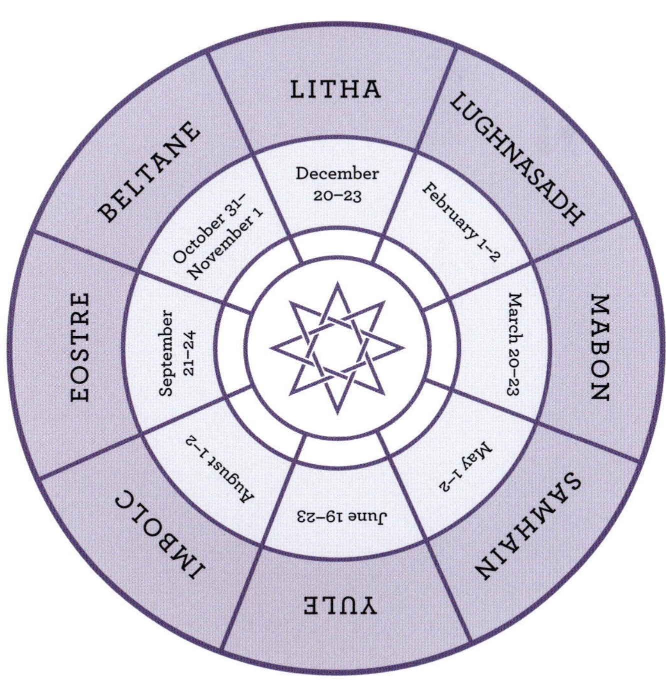

# MONTH ONE: PREPARATION

Use this month to get yourself organized in preparation for the year ahead.

These tasks and rituals can be performed during the course of the month—it's not necessary to do everything at once. Concentrate on the inner meaning of each task as you perform it and keep a record of your thoughts and activities on the page opposite.

## SPELLS

- **At the start of the month:**

"I entreat your blessings, Mother Earth:
On this, the first day of my magical life,
Bless the path I walk,
Bless my endeavors,
Let me only do those things that usher in good,
And keep me safe from harm.
So might it be."

- **At the start of each ritual:**

"Let me be powerful and wise.
Let me be true and strong.
Let me love and be loved.
So might it be."

**SEE ALSO:**

Witchcraft Basics, pp. 20–37

Getting Started, pp. 80–83

## ACTIVITIES

- Create your Book of Shadows. Write rituals of your own: one to dedicate it, and another to use when updating it. Take a little time at the end of the month to reflect on the nature of your path, and note your thoughts in your book.
- Prepare your altar, and light a candle to dedicate it. If your altar is outside, place the candle in a garden lantern.
- Prepare your tools, and dedicate them to their tasks. Fill your chalice with water to drink at the end of the ritual, and dedicate it to the water of life.
- If you decide to wear something special for rituals and festivals, now is the time to choose or make it. You may like to have different clothing for use indoors and outdoors, and for cold weather or hot weather. Keeping them only for wear for this practice adds to the ceremonial aspect of the path.

## YOUR MONTH

Use this chart to log the activities you carry out this month. Make notes at the end to record how they influenced your day-to-day life.

**My chosen Path**

**My Book of Shadows dedication ritual**

**My Book of Shadows writing ritual**

**Location of my altar**

**My ritual clothing**

**What have I learned about myself this month?**

# MONTH TWO: IMBOLC

The sabbat of Imbolc marks the start of the new year for practitioners of the Craft; this is a time for cleaning everything—body, mind, and spirit!

These tasks and rituals can be performed during the course of the month—it's not necessary to do everything at once. Concentrate on the inner meaning of each task as you perform it and keep a record of your thoughts and activities on the page opposite.

## SPELLS

- **For cleaning the home:**

  "Hail, Great Mother!
  Be with me on this day of spring's awakening.
  As I clean my home, may I cleanse my spirit and my mind.
  So I may honor you, this world, and myself.
  So might it be!"

- **For changing a bad habit**

  "I am but small in the world, and flawed.
  But I know I can do more, be more.
  Goddess grant me the strength to change this habit,
  Transform it into something good,
  As I turn myself into something good.
  So let it be."

**SEE ALSO:**

Imbolc, pp. 54–55

Imbolc Activities, pp. 106–107

## ACTIVITIES

- Clean your home. Make it a thorough cleaning, with windows wide open. Make any repairs that you've been putting off: oil that squeaky hinge, stick down that peeling wallpaper, touch up that chipped paint. Mend any favorite or ceremonial clothes that have got a little battered.
- Consider a new haircut or makeup, if you wear it, or a new exercise regime to improve your fitness and stamina.
- Take the time to examine yourself. Are you holding on to any old anger or slights? Any old bad habits or outdated routines? Would you be happier if you let them go?
- Make a talisman. If you can't make it yourself, search out a piece of jewelry that speaks to you of the season, and treat yourself. Or make yourself a Brigid Cross.
- Consider your altar. Can you do anything to make it more personal this month?

## YOUR MONTH

Use this chart to log the activities you carry out this month. Make notes at the end to record how they influenced your day-to-day life.

**Chosen Path activities**

______________________________

______________________________

______________________________

**Changes to appearance**

______________________________

______________________________

______________________________

**Old habits/routines stopped**

______________________________

______________________________

______________________________

**My talisman**

______________________________

______________________________

______________________________

**Changes to my altar**

______________________________

______________________________

______________________________

**What have I learned about myself this month?**

______________________________

______________________________

______________________________

# MONTH THREE: EOSTRE

The world is waking properly from its winter sleep; now is the time to get out and reacquaint yourself with the natural world.

These tasks and rituals can be performed during the course of the month—it's not necessary to do everything at once. Concentrate on the inner meaning of each task as you perform it and keep a record of your thoughts and activities on the page opposite.

## SPELLS

- **For greeting wild animals:**

"Merry meet, Great Mother!
Grant me the gentleness, the quietness,
To greet the little ones of your world;
Without harm, without fear, may they regard me.
Greetings, small creatures.
I thank you for brightening my life with your presence.
Blessed be!"

- **For the Threefold Goddess:**

"Hail, Threefold Goddess.
Grant me a vision of yourself,
That I may honor and remember you
In all my actions and my words.
Let me only act to honor you.
Let me be true and strong.
Let me love and be loved.
So might it be."

**SEE ALSO:**

Eostre, pp. 56–57

Eostre Activities, pp. 108–109

## ACTIVITIES

- Get out and about. Visit parks, woods, and rivers. Stretch your arms, legs and back, and breathe deeply. Watch birds in flight, look for hares in the fields, and see if you can spot fish in rivers.
- Indulge yourself with your favorite treat. Describe in detail how it tastes and how it makes you feel. See if you can recreate the experience in your mind.
- Sit quietly and meditate on the Threefold Goddess. What does she look like? What does she sound like? What color is her hair, her eyes, her skin? What is she wearing? Note down or draw your image of her in your Book of Shadows.
- Create a spell of your own, something to express your thanks for how you feel, or your wish for things to improve. Speak it silently on waking and before sleeping.

## YOUR MONTH

Use this chart to log the activities you carry out this month. Make notes at the end to record how they influenced your day-to-day life.

**Chosen Path activities**

______________________________

______________________________

______________________________

**Places visited**

______________________________

______________________________

______________________________

**Wildlife encountered**

______________________________

______________________________

______________________________

**Favorite treat**

______________________________

______________________________

______________________________

**My Eostre spell**

______________________________

______________________________

______________________________

**What have I learned about myself this month?**

______________________________

______________________________

______________________________

# MONTH FOUR: TIME FOR ACTION

You are now a quarter of the way through the year; the quieter, gentler sabbats of Imbolc and Eostre are behind you, and it's time to prepare for more activity-based times.

These tasks and rituals can be performed during the course of the month—it's not necessary to do everything at once. Concentrate on the inner meaning of each task as you perform it and keep a record of your thoughts and activities on the page opposite.

## SPELLS

- **For blessing seeds:**

  "Goddess, God, and Green Man,
  Bless these seeds I scatter.
  May they grow strong and healthy,
  And grant their strength and
  health to all who touch them."
  So might it be."

- **For using harvested fruits**

  "I thank you, Mother Goddess,
  Father God,
  For your generosity and goodness,
  For the bounty of these fruits,
  For their health, their flavor,
  their goodness.
  May we never forget that they
  come from you.
  Blessed be."

**SEE ALSO:**

The Role of Nature, pp. 24–27

Embracing Nature, pp. 84–87

## ACTIVITIES

- If you've been sedentary for the past few months, now is the time to start going out walking, running, or cycling to build up some stamina for the summer. Silently chant the name of the god or the goddess as you do so. Make the action an act of salutation.
- Make plans for the coming summer. Is there a favorite summer location you'd like to revisit? Ensure you have everything you need for warmer weather. Check your wardrobe.
- Ensure everything is ready in your garden, windowbox, or plant pots. Weed, clean, top dress, and water, then bless the plants and seeds within them!
- Pick and harvest any early summer fruits or herbs and use them in your meals.
- Decide how you are going to decorate your altar over the next few months. Collect the supplies you'll need.

## YOUR MONTH

Use this chart to log the activities you carry out this month. Make notes at the end to record how they influenced your day-to-day life.

**Chosen Path activities**

______________________________

______________________________

______________________________

**Outdoor activity**

______________________________

______________________________

______________________________

**Summer plans**

______________________________

______________________________

______________________________

**Fruitful harvest**

______________________________

______________________________

______________________________

**Changes to my altar**

______________________________

______________________________

______________________________

**What have I learned about myself this month?**

______________________________

______________________________

______________________________

# MONTH FIVE: BELTANE

May Day is a good time to start new projects, especially out of doors; think about green witch activities and those relating to the sabbat for inspiration.

These tasks and rituals can be performed during the course of the month—it's not necessary to do everything at once. Concentrate on the inner meaning of each task as you perform it and keep a record of your thoughts and activities on the page opposite.

## SPELLS

- **For blessing a new project:**

  "As I set forth on this project,
  Great Mother,
  Grant me patience and skill.
  Let my hands be steady,
  My eyes precise,
  My mind collected and calm,
  And let me succeed.
  So might it be."

- **For combatting loneliness:**

  "Let me turn this loneliness
  into solitude.
  Let me find peace in your presence,
  Great Mother,
  Console me, I entreat you,
  Let me turn this loneliness into
  opportunity, to befriend myself
  and find a way to ease the world.
  So might it be."

**SEE ALSO:**

Beltane,
pp. 58–59

Beltane Activities,
pp. 110–111

## ACTIVITIES

- Welcome the sun every morning. It does not need to be at sunrise every day, but try to make it at that time once a week for the whole of this month.
- Explore outdoors. Find somewhere new you can reach easily and visit it. Take photos or draw pictures. Collect sticks or flowers. Listen to birdsong and the rustling of leaves. Focus on the joyful, uplifting power of the natural world.
- Decide on your project for the month—or the year if you choose to plant something and watch it grow. It should be something relevant to Beltane. For example, learn about the sun, our local star, or study the Beltane practices of yesteryear, or write a series of little poems for your loved ones.
- If you find yourself feeling lonely, consider what you can do to alleviate it. Is there a group of like-minded people nearby that you can arrange to meet up with?

## YOUR MONTH

Use this chart to log the activities you carry out this month. Make notes at the end to record how they influenced your day-to-day life.

**Chosen Path activities**

____________________
____________________
____________________

**Sunrise location**

____________________
____________________
____________________

**New destination**

____________________
____________________
____________________

**Project for the month**

____________________
____________________
____________________

**Group joined**

____________________
____________________
____________________

**What have I learned about myself this month?**

____________________
____________________
____________________

# MONTH SIX: LITHA

The Summer solstice is a good time for considering what you have achieved so far this year, and for gathering your forces for the months to come.

These tasks and rituals can be performed during the course of the month—it's not necessary to do everything at once. Concentrate on the inner meaning of each task as you perform it and keep a record of your thoughts and activities on the page opposite.

## SPELLS

- **To aid learning:**

  "Merry meet, Great Goddess, Great God.
  Grant me the patience to listen
    with intent
  To the language of the birds.
  Let me recognize it, learn it,
  That I may know when they are in
    distress and do what I can to help.
  Let me take that knowledge with me
    into other fields,
  That I may learn how to understand
    your world.
  So might it be."

- **For sunflower growth:**

  "Grow for me, small seed, I entreat you,
  Grow tall and strong and bless the world
    with your sunshine.
  So let it be!"

**See also:**

Litha,
pp. 60–61

Litha Activities,
pp. 112–113

## ACTIVITIES

- Seek out a new landscape, even if it means traveling farther afield—somewhere coastal, mountainous, rural, or lakeside. Bring a memento back—a pebble, a leaf, a postcard—something that will evoke memories of the visit.
- Create your own dedication for the summer. Make it rhyme!
- Learn to recognize local birdsong. See if you can find any local bird watchers or twitchers to help you.
- Plant sunflower seeds. Tend them over the next year and see how tall they grow.
- Have you found any natural activities or wild creatures that make you particularly happy? Try to include them in your life more often.

## YOUR MONTH

Use this chart to log the activities you carry out this month. Make notes at the end to record how they influenced your day-to-day life.

**Chosen Path activities**

**New landscape**

**Summer dedication**

**Birdsong**

**Activity/creature**

**What have I learned about myself this month?**

# MONTH SEVEN: TAKE A BREATH

You're halfway through the year, and the days are becoming shorter as you head toward winter; it's time to pause and consider what you've accomplished, and what you still need to learn.

These tasks and rituals can be performed during the course of the month—it's not necessary to do everything at once. Concentrate on the inner meaning of each task as you perform it and keep a record of your thoughts and activities on the page opposite.

## SPELLS

- **For taking a pause:**

  "Grant me rest, Great Goddess.
  Let me gather my strength for the coming months.
  Let me reflect on what I have learned,
  And look forward with joy to what is yet to be learned.
  But first, grant me rest, and let me lie
  Content in your love.
  So might it be."

- **For blessing fruitfulness:**

  "Blessed be, Great Goddess,
  Blessed be, Great God.
  I praise and honor you for your bounty,
  Your fruitfulness, and the glory of your light.
  Blessed be!"

**SEE ALSO:**

The Green Witch, pp. 70–71

Growth of a Green Witch, pp. 122–123

## ACTIVITIES

- Group-orientated activities are very much a feature of the fall and winter festivals. Plan how you're going to celebrate in line with your Path, and reach out to loved ones with invitations.
- Spend time outdoors, in the garden or a local park or wood if you can. Go in the early morning when it's quiet and create your own salutation to the sun. Say it—silently if you prefer—while you contemplate all the good things of summer.
- Harvest any fruits, vegetables, and herbs that are ready. Prepare any for freezing or storing for future use.
- Learn a new recipe or two using seasonal produce. Praise the goddess for her fruitfulness, and the god for his light.
- Decide how to decorate your altar for the coming months.

## YOUR MONTH

Use this chart to log the activities you carry out this month. Make notes at the end to record how they influenced your day-to-day life.

**Chosen Path activities**

______________________

______________________

______________________

**Festival plans**

______________________

______________________

______________________

**Sun salutation**

______________________

______________________

______________________

**Late-summer harvest**

______________________

______________________

______________________

**Changes to my altar**

______________________

______________________

______________________

**What have I learned about myself this month?**

______________________

______________________

______________________

# MONTH EIGHT: LUGHNASADH

The height of summer is ideal for taking pleasure in all you have achieved so far this year; rest for a while and enjoy the sunshine.

These tasks and rituals can be performed during the course of the month—it's not necessary to do everything at once. Concentrate on the inner meaning of each task as you perform it and keep a record of your thoughts and activities on the page opposite.

## SPELLS

- **For seeing things anew:**
  (face east, arms outspread)

"Light of the Morning, of the rising sun,
Bless me with brightness, let my mind be clear
To see all things anew.
Let me be open and understanding,
Open to truth, and understanding of difference.
So let it be."

- **For contemplating things past:**
  (face west, arms crossed over chest)

"Light of the Evening, of the setting sun,
Bless me with compassion and remembrance.
Let me appreciate all I have learned,
And put it to good use in the future.
Blessed be."

**SEE ALSO:**

Lughnasadh, pp. 62–63

Lughnasadh Activities, pp. 114–115

## ACTIVITIES

- Return to a favorite outdoor space and see what changes have taken place since you were last there. Can you learn anything from them?
- Listen to your favorite music while contemplating what summer means to you now, and what it has meant in the past. Record your thoughts in your Book of Shadows.
- Have a barbecue! It's the ideal urban replacement for the Lughnasadh bonfire. Invite friends and family—ask them to bring provisions if they're happy to do so—and have a joyful, happy, tasty time.
- Sing! Old favorites or new, by yourself or with others, indoors or out. It's the perfect way to celebrate the season.
- Choose a plant or two to grow at home. Learn all you can about them—how they evolved, their native environment, any medicinal or culinary qualities they possess.

## YOUR MONTH

Use this chart to log the activities you carry out this month. Make notes at the end to record how they influenced your day-to-day life.

**Chosen Path activities**

______________________________

______________________________

______________________________

**Favorite outdoor space**

______________________________

______________________________

______________________________

**Music**

______________________________

______________________________

______________________________

**Barbecue menu**

______________________________

______________________________

______________________________

**Plant project**

______________________________

______________________________

______________________________

**What have I learned about myself this month?**

______________________________

______________________________

______________________________

# MONTH NINE: MABON

The beginning of fall is the time to step back and take stock of where you are and what you've achieved so far this year—and to celebrate with friends and family.

These tasks and rituals can be performed during the course of the month—it's not necessary to do everything at once. Concentrate on the inner meaning of each task as you perform it and keep a record of your thoughts and activities on the page opposite.

**SEE ALSO:**

Mabon, pp. 64–65

Mabon Activities, pp. 116–117

## SPELLS

- **For contemplating the cycle of life:**

"Blessed be, Corn King, God of the harvest now at rest
Until your rebirth next spring.
Blessed be, Mother Goddess, nurturer, bearer of the future.
Grant me your grace to live with the seasons,
Grow and increase, sow and release, and age slowly into wisdom.
So might it be."

- **For dedicating work to the Goddess:**

"Bless me, great Goddess, and let me ever put you first in everything I do,
That our beautiful world may be healthy and safe,
That I and all around me may reap the benefits of a happy world.
So might it be."

## ACTIVITIES

- Gather fallen leaves to lay on your altar, or make pictures with them. Contemplate the cycle of birth, growth, death, rebirth that makes Earth the wonderful ever-changing planet that it is.
- Eat an apple every day. Eat other fruit, too, both native and foreign. Which do you prefer, and why?
- List three accomplishments for this year: cooking, reading, writing, acting, drawing, walking, cycling, helping charities, helping friends, neighbors, strangers—all count toward making your life richer.
- Plant some bulbs. Use your Book of Shadow to record how they grow—when they first appear above the ground, when they flower, how long they live.
- Think about what fall means to you, then design your vision of the spirit of fall, in any manner and medium you like. Place it on your altar and dedicate it to the goddess.

## YOUR MONTH

Use this chart to log the activities you carry out this month. Make notes at the end to record how they influenced your day-to-day life.

**Chosen Path activities**

________________________________________

________________________________________

________________________________________

**Favorite fruit**

________________________________________

________________________________________

________________________________________

**Accomplishments**

________________________________________

________________________________________

________________________________________

**Bulbs planted**

________________________________________

________________________________________

________________________________________

**Spirit vision**

________________________________________

________________________________________

________________________________________

**What have I learned about myself this month?**

________________________________________

________________________________________

________________________________________

# MONTH TEN: TIME TO REFLECT

You are now into fall, with its shorter days and longer nights; it's a time to reflect on the joys and sorrows of the months gone by, and to consider what you could have done differently.

These tasks and rituals can be performed during the course of the month—it's not necessary to do everything at once. Concentrate on the inner meaning of each task as you perform it and keep a record of your thoughts and activities on the page opposite.

## SPELLS

- **For baking bread:**

"I have made the dough, and kneaded it
And left it to rise
For the yeast to work its magic.
I have made it with love, and shall bake it with love.
May those who eat it know it was made with love,
And find satisfaction, health, and contentment in its taste.
So might it be!"

- **For the willpower to break a habit:**

"Hail, Mother Earth, who guards and cares for me.
I thank you for your help thus far.
May my work to beat this habit bear fruit and be successful.
So might it be."

**See also:**

The Kitchen Witch, pp. 72–73

The Craft of the Kitchen Witch, pp. 124–125

## YOUR MONTH

Use this chart to log the activities you carry out this month. Make notes at the end to record how they influenced your day-to-day life.

**Chosen Path activities**

**Favorite tradition**

**Favorite deity**

**Outdoor plans**

**Plant of the year**

**What have I learned about myself this month?**

## ACTIVITIES

- How much have you learned about the Path? Do you understand its traditions and practices, and how to best use them? What are your favorites?
- What have you learned about the deities and their different aspects? Do you have a favorite, and if so, why?
- How has your growing space performed this year? What's grown best? What would you like to try next spring?
- Try your hand at making bread. It's a fascinating process, and gives a new insight into, and appreciation of, this basic food. Choose an easy recipe. If you enjoy the process, try again with something more complex.
- What discoveries have you made about yourself? Have you been able to get rid of habits or routines that served no purpose? Do you have a healthier, happier lifestyle? What would improve matters in the coming year?

# MONTH ELEVEN: SAMHAIN

Summer finally draws to a close—this turning of the year marks a time to contemplate the cycle of life and death.

These tasks and rituals can be performed during the course of the month—it's not necessary to do everything at once. Concentrate on the inner meaning of each task as you perform it and keep a record of your thoughts and activities on the page opposite.

## SPELLS

- **To honor the deceased:**

  "[Name], I honor you today and all days.
  May I never forget your life, may I never forget all you meant
  To those of us who loved you.
  Sleep softly in the Summerland, until we meet again.
  Blessed be."

- **For contemplating death:**

  "The wheel ever turns, all is reborn to live and die and live again.
  From seed to flower to seed to earth,
  From acorn to oak to acorn to earth,
  May the wonders of the cycle of life and time never cease.
  Blessed be."

**SEE ALSO:**

Samhain, pp. 66–67

Samhain Activities, pp. 118–119

## ACTIVITIES

- Eat a toffee apple slowly, savoring the taste. Consider the marriage of sweet and sour. What other foods with "opposite" taste sensations can you try?
- Go for walks as often as you can. Enjoy the changeable weather. Wear an orange or purple scarf.
- Take a day to honor the deceased. Visit their graves, say a quiet hail and farewell and be resolved to meet with them again when the time is right.
- Invite friends and family for a meal, and talk about lost loved ones. Raise a toast to them. Afterward, play the music they liked, or watch an old favorite movie. End the event with a salutation to them.
- Light a candle and meditate on the cycle of life and death.

## YOUR MONTH

Use this chart to log the activities you carry out this month. Make notes at the end to record how they influenced your day-to-day life.

**Chosen Path activities**

____________________

____________________

____________________

**Taste sensation**

____________________

____________________

____________________

**Favorite walk**

____________________

____________________

____________________

**Graves visited**

____________________

____________________

____________________

**Deceased honored**

____________________

____________________

____________________

**What have I learned about myself this month?**

____________________

____________________

____________________

# MONTH TWELVE: YULE

Warmth and happy revelry on the longest night of the year to welcome the returning sun!

These tasks and rituals can be performed during the course of the month—it's not necessary to do everything at once. Concentrate on the inner meaning of each task as you perform it and keep a record of your thoughts and activities on the page opposite.

## SPELLS

- **To bless presents as you wrap:**

  "Hail, Holly King, at this time of year
  When we rejoice at the Sun God's return from the night!
  Let this gift bring pleasure and delight to [name],
  May they think of me kindly when opening it!
  So might it be!"

- **For protecting winter birds:**

  "Great Mother, as I provide food for your birds
  At this cold and needy time of year,
  Protect them, I beg you. Help them find shelter, keep them safe through the cold and dark,
  Until they greet the spring with their song once again.
  So might it be."

**SEE ALSO:**

Yule, pp. 68–69

Yule Activities, pp. 120–121

## ACTIVITIES

- Send cards to everyone, if that's your tradition—physical cards and/or e-cards. Wish everyone the happiest of Yuletides and let them know they are in your thoughts.
- Buy or make gifts. They can be as large or as small as you like, but thought should go into their choice. They should be something you know the person wants or needs. Bless each one as you wrap it.
- Decorate a Yule tree. Choose decorations that reflect your Path. If you don't have a tree for the house (or even if you do), find one outside and decorate it with food the birds will love!
- Enjoy a feast with loved ones. Simple but tasty is always better than extravagant and stressful.
- Go outside with friends after dark to admire the midwinter sky. What constellations can you see?

## YOUR MONTH

Use this chart to log the activities you carry out this month. Make notes at the end to record how they influenced your day-to-day life.

**Chosen Path activities**

____________________

____________________

____________________

**Cards sent**

____________________

____________________

____________________

**Gifts made**

____________________

____________________

____________________

**Favorite decoration**

____________________

____________________

____________________

**Constellation**

____________________

____________________

____________________

**What have I learned about myself this month?**

____________________

____________________

____________________

# INDEX

## ABOUT THE AUTHOR

**Alestrel Evergreen**—eclectic witch with a penchant for music, cosmic, and sigil magic. Also exceptionally good with growing things.

## PICTURE CREDITS

**Alamy Stock Photo:** Steve Sant 41. **Noun Project** line illustrations: "See also" eye used throughout the book Creative Art; Nawicon 27(t), 87; Travis Avery 28; Kameo Gregson 34–35; Olena Panasovska 38, 75(t), 76, 105; Avana Vana 48(t), 50(t), 77, 103(b); Adrian Coquet 52; ahmad 74; Visualeat 75(b), 113(t); andriwidodo 81; Made x Made 83(t), 91(b), 109; Rockicon 83(b); barurezeki 85; Adam Robinson 89; Ardi Nurfiyanto 91(t), 103(t), 113(b), 127; Timo Schmid 99; chappara 101; Muhammad Auns 107; Vectors Point 111; Chanut is Industries 115; Nook Fulloption 119; fae frey 121; prasong tadoungsom 123; Okasana Latysheva 124 (ear, nose); Basti Steinhauer 124 (mouth); asianson.design 124 (touch); Ben Davis 124 (eye), 129; Guilherme Furtado 125. **Pexels:** Anna Shvets 13(t); Kevin Bidwell 15; Tomas Anunziata 25; Nadi Lindsay 27; Rodnae-productions 35, 89, 102; Seyfi Durmaz 54; Brett Sayles 55(tl); Pixabay 55(bl), 113; Nastyasensei 55(r); Belle Co 56; Eva Elijas 57(r); Leigh Patrick 61(tl); Suzy Hazelwood 67(br); Skyler Ewing 69(r); Ylanite Koppens 81; Cottonbro 88; Daniela Constantini 90; Tara Winstead 100; Jill Burrow 107(b); Jill Wellington 110, 120; Jasmine Carter 111; Michael Burrows 116; Kindel Media 121; Jessica Lewis 134. **Pixabay:** Amber_Avalona 10; WikiImages 24; HNewberry 29; Shedon 30; acekreations 42; Bru-nO 53; Illuvis 57(tl); leswhalley 59(tr); Carola69 59(br); Hans 60, 65(tl); suju-foto 61(bl); Capri23auto 61(tr), 71; gate74 61(br); Elstef 63(bl); congerdesign 63(bc), 65(bl), 66; Anestiev 63(br); mploscar 64; MabelAmber 65(br); monicore (67bl); mbll 68; TizzleBDizzle 69(bl); wagrati_photo 95; Pezibear 107(t); ulleo 115; Amber_Avalona 119(t); Marjattacajan 124; Angela_Yuriko_Smith 128; pixel2013 136; sweetlouise 140; TimHill 142; IndiraFoto 144; HelgaKa 148; pexels 154; PenjaK 156. **Shutterstock:** Nadezhda Shuparskaia (opener) 18–19, 78–79, 130–131; RAphoto77 32; ju_see 33, 111; Riccardo Mayer 40(t); Zvereva Yana 50(b); Carol Blaker 51; Karina Bostanika 77; Purple Clouds 92(t); Viktor Petkov 92(b); Dan Kosmayer 93(t); Anton Starikov 93(b); Africa Studio 104. **Unsplash:** Yeshi Kangrang 2; Eli Defaria 12; Katherine Hanlon 83; Michaela 13(b); Ksenia Yakovleva 14, 23; Karina Vorozheeva 20; Tamara Menzi 21, 122; Bogdan Todoran 22; Jonathan Kemper 26, 86, 114; Robert Lukeman 31; Rachel Sandu 36; Jessica Furtney 37; Foad Roshan 38(t); Daphne 38(b); Gabriel Jimenez 40(b); Claire Gray 44; Christin Hume 46; Vincent van Zalinge 57(bl); Kevin Wolf 58; Lucinda Hershberger 59(l); Nadine Redlich 62; Devi Puspita Amartha Yahya 63(t); Andre Ouellet 65(tr); Shelley Pauls 67(tl); Ing W 67(tr); Hannah Pemberton 69(tl); Erda Estremera 70; Annie Spratt 72; Vincent Ledvina 74; Ganapathy Kumar Ve 75; Paolo Nicolello 80; Juan Cortes 82; Christian Widell 84; Jamie Street 87; Sierra Nicole Narvaeth 91; Anup Ghag 94; Alice Pasqual 98; Raphael Renter 106; Dieny Portinanni 108; Sara Codair 109; Lyle Hastie 112; Julian Ackroyd 117(l); Anna Kaminova 117(r); Erik Witsoe 118; Freestocks 119(b); Raspopova Marina 123; Melissa Mullin 126; Tina Witherspoon 127; Miriam Espacio 129; Gary Bendig 138; Markus Spiske 146; Greg Shield 150; Ben Garratt 152.

Every effort has been made to trace the copyright holders of material featured in this book. If application is made in writing to the publisher, any omissions will be included in future editions.